AN HOUR WITH JESUS

Abbé Gaston Courtois

An Hour with Jesus

Meditations for Religious

SECOND SERIES

Translated from the French by
SISTER HELEN MADELEINE, S.N.D.

THE NEWMAN PRESS
Westminster, Maryland
1957

First published, 1956
Second printing, 1957

Originally published in France as L'HEURE DE JÉSUS, *copyright 1953 by Éditions Fleurus.*

Nihil Obstat: The Right Reverend THOMAS J. RILEY
Censor Librorum

Imprimatur: The Most Reverend RICHARD J. CUSHING, D.D.
Archbishop of Boston
Boston, March 31, 1955

Letter of the Most Reverend Pierre Brot, Auxiliary Bishop of Paris

Reverend Father,

You were very kind to send me the text of the second volume of *An Hour with Jesus*.

Let me thank you for the powerful help which you bring thus to consecrated souls who are eager to deepen their interior life.

I am confident that they will appreciate the profound thoughts which you propose for their reflection; they will be strengthened in the spirit of faith, remembering that "while putting into practice the truth one knows, one merits that which one knows not." They will understand better that, for them, "the ideal should be to live naturally in the supernatural"!

How much profit consecrated souls will be able to derive from the beautiful chapter in which you exhort them to "Silence, Our Strength": that silence "without which one lives, as it were, on the surface of the soul"; that silence "which gives solidarity to the words that we say"; that silence "which is not God, but in which the Father speaks the Eternal Word, His Son, and the Word exists."

In honesty, loyalty, and humility, these consecrated souls will contribute their "Royal Service" as true daughters of the Church, as devoted missionaries.

I hope that this book, so rich in instruction, will receive the welcome it deserves, not only from the religious for whom it is intended primarily, but from those souls in the world who are striving for perfection.

Reverend Father, please accept the expression of my sincere devotedness in our Saviour and in our Mother Mary.

PIERRE BROT
Bishop of Marciana,
Auxiliary of Paris

Contents

AN HOUR WITH JESUS

CHAPTER I

The Spirit of Faith

For men in the Middle Ages all the realities of the universe were filled with God. Our modern world is a technical world where nothing refers to the Sacred Presence, a world where that only is real which is the result of experience.

Hence the importance, at this moment more than ever, of living evidence of genuine faith, to which consecrated souls particularly should contribute. It is supremely necessary at this time to educate Christian boys and girls in such a way that they will be sincere examples of supernatural living.

It is important, then, to meditate often on the spirit of faith, that we may increase faith in our own lives and be able to develop it in the souls of those of whom we have charge.

Meditation

At the beginning of this meditation let us adore our Lord who begs an act of faith from all those who approach Him. Let us read again in the Gospels the numerous texts referring to faith. No cures are mentioned in the Scriptures which are not the result of an expression of faith. Jesus referred to that fact often.

He asks an explicit act of faith from the father in anguish before the cure of his child (Mark 9:23); and of Martha as she wept before the raising of Lazarus (John 11:26). This faith He holds up for the admiration of all at the home of the centurion (Matt. 8:10), and at the home of the Canaanite (Matt. 15:28). From His Apostles He asks a total faith, without reserve, without measure (Matt. 8:26, 14:31, 16:8; Mark 14:40; John 20:29). One feels it is a point that He insists on in their training.

Let us also give ourselves to be molded by Jesus, and in the silence of prayer, let us listen to Him. Let us be completely docile to His interior action. To help us therein, we can make use of the thoughts in the following pages. They have no other purpose than to serve as points of departure for the divine colloquy, for, after all, it is the Master alone who teaches and fashions the soul.

To believe is to share in the knowledge of God; it is to

cling to the truths revealed by the Church. Still more, it is to adhere to a Person who is Truth itself, the substantial Truth, the only One who has a right to say: "I am the Truth."

For purposes of study, of analysis, of doctrinal explanation, theologians have distinguished three theological virtues. This trilogy, however, is only the triple expression of a unique reality: our life in relation to God in the earthly phase of our existence.

In this life there is no true faith without hope and charity. There is no hope without faith and love. There is no love without faith and hope.

In heaven charity will have absorbed everything, for there will be no shadow to replace faith. Hope will have made its way to the goal so longed for. Love alone will remain, love which will receive and will give itself in exchange without shadow and without restraint.

It is only on this earth that we can live by faith. Let us profit by this fact. Later, it will be too late. It is only on this earth that we can live by hope. Only here can our love be meritorious.

Our degree of glory in heaven will be exactly that of our life of grace at the hour of death.

"The religious vocation," says Canon Leclercq, "supposes that God is perceived as a personal Being, a living Being, with whom our relations are as person to person."[1] If we do not live our lives according to faith, the religious life is an absurdity. The religious soul can expand only in proportion as it believes in the invisible, as it studies the invisible, as it works for the invisible, that is to say: in proportion as it grows in faith.

It is normal that on earth our faith should be tried; otherwise how would it be meritorious? "Faith," said St. John of the Cross, "means seeing God face to face in darkness; possessing Him though He is hidden."

Edmond Rostand said: "It is night wherein it is pleasant to think of light."

The Abbé Perreyve said: "In divine truths there is light enough for reasonable belief; there is darkness enough for faith to be meritorious and a virtue. If there were more light, faith would no longer be justified in being called meritorious."

Père Perroy adds: "We always want someone who will converse with us: but the Infant of Bethlehem was silent like all children. Christ on the altar, under the form of bread, is silent. Without this silence where would be the merit of our faith? If our eyes saw God, if our ears heard Him, we would not be putting our faith in God, but in ourselves." [2]

According to the word of Père Chevrier: "Because there are so many reasoners, there are so few saints."

This is what St. Vincent de Paul, with his great, good, supernatural sense and his experience with souls, used to say: "The more one turns his eyes to look at the sun, the less he sees; likewise, the more one tries to reason about the truths of religion, the less he knows by faith."

In order to grow in faith must we not before all else make a loyal effort to act in conformity with faith? When one lives according to the truth one knows, one merits what one does not know.

Our Lord has said so well: "He who does the truth

[that is to say, he who acts in conformity with the truth] comes to the light" (John 3:21).

Père Robert de Langeac wrote:

Consider the soul living by faith. When it goes to pray it enters without hesitation into the inner sanctuary, where God, abiding in the Trinity of His Persons, gives Himself to it. Here it adores, praises, loves, listens to God, speaks to Him. It even seeks to take part in His intimate divine life, creature-fashion, speaking with the Father His Word, breathing forth the Spirit of Love proceeding from Father and Son, returning with this divine Spirit to Father and Son . . .

. . . See the difference between a soul of mediocre faith, and one that is quietly and unpretentiously convinced of the value of silence, of the power of recollection, of the possibility of intimate union with God. The first soul drags itself along, the other flies and becomes more and more pleasing to God, because it not merely hears but heeds His voice. If we would please Him, then, a simple penetrating faith must fill our souls; by its light must we judge events both pleasant and unpleasant. All our spiritual slackening is the result of a lack of faith; when we feel we have relaxed, when we have become less recollected, less mortified, less generous in God's service, then it is with this foundation, the spirit of faith, that we must begin the reform. Instead of being led by mere reason, or sometimes even by sense-impressions, we must use our faith to rectify these sources of action.[3]

When activity does not spring from faith, and when faith is employed only in certain circumstances, then the motives of action are only motives of a natural order. In reality it is egotism, more or less crafty, it is self-seeking, it is the satisfaction of the senses, it is self-love, the desire to excel, to dazzle, to succeed. It is the urge to organize, to profit, to command. It is neither pure love of God nor of neighbor. What makes all this the more deplorable is that such persons are deluded. One can raise a lot of dust, but that is not constructing anything; one can produce much smoke, but that is not producing heat; one can make a lot of noise, but that is not accomplishing any good.

Colloquy

My daughter, never forget the word of My Apostle: "The just man liveth by faith." A religious should permeate with the spirit of faith whatever task is confided to her. Otherwise she is merely a hireling; she is no longer a religious.

If you do not choose Me to direct your activities, if you do not have Me in view, if you do not direct to Me your apostolate, if you do not work for Me, you build on sand.

Be more concerned about Me, about what I think, about what I desire. Be concerned about *My* concerns, and I will busy Myself about yours. Be less concerned about visible results than about eternal values. I give the increase and fruitfulness in proportion as you permit Me to act in you and by you.

Think more often of My presence. Seek Me in the souls around you. Act in My presence. Speak in My presence. But above all, listen to Me in silence. Try more often to understand what I think of your words, of your attitudes, of your decisions. Enjoy the intimacy of My kingdom, the kingdom of My thoughts, the kingdom of My virtues, the kingdom of My love, and all the rest will be added unto you.

When you lack the spirit of faith, you paralyze Me. I am obliged then to leave you to your poor human ways. And then you come to naught: a little blaze, with much smoke . . .

When you animate your work with supernatural motives, when the Gospel becomes in you spirit and life, when you pray with My prayer, when you speak with My words, when you love with My heart, when you efface yourself and give Me precedence, when you try to draw souls to Me, and do Me the honor of believing that I am more attractive than all the trifles to which you attach too much importance, then I can work, then I can make souls feel My love. I can realize very well what seems impossible to you with your short-sighted human views.

When will you understand the power of My grace? If you had faith, even the size of a mustard seed, you could move mountains, you would live more with the invisible than with the visible, you would discover Me in everyone, and you would have a supernatural intuition of what goes on in their hearts.

If you had faith, you would never feel alone. You would find Me within yourself, near you, with you. You would understand the price of life and the price of death, the part played by the cross and the richness of suffering.

If you had faith, everything would be a grace for you and a reason for thanksgiving; everything would be a joy and a motive for rejoicing.

If you had faith, the Mass would be the focal point of your days, the Sacred Host would draw forth a burst of love from your soul, and you would marvel at the power you have over My Heart.

You give yourself too much to worldly activity. With Me everything is simple, even the apostolate; if you come to Me, you will lack nothing for the souls which I have confided to you. Human means will be given to you, but because you will have given first place to the things of the soul, these other needs will assume a secondary role. I will take care of them, and they will become channels of grace instead of obstacles.

You can rely on Me only if I am truly for you someone who counts, someone on whom you depend. You are a religious only insofar as you rely on Me, only insofar as you refer to Me in all things.

I expect from you, My daughter, a living faith, an ardent faith, a sincere faith, a militant faith, a courageous faith.

It is particularly in the time of trial that I can gauge your spirit of faith. Do not be surprised if from time to time I permit suffering. Then it is that you are most apostolic, that you procure for Me that serum of meritorious faith which permits Me to guide the souls who are groping and to cure the souls who are in doubt.

Ask Me for faith, ask Me for the spirit of faith, ask Me for an abiding spirit of faith. That is a petition which I grant always.

Above all, ask Me for much love. The more you will love with My heart, the more you will see with My eyes.

Examen

1. Is my faith truly warm and radiant?

2. Is my faith a total adhesion to Christ and to the Church, without reserve, without measure, with my whole soul? "Christ and the Church are one," said Joan of Arc. "He who hears you, hears me," said Jesus to His apostles.

3. Is the presence of God familiar to me? Is God really *Someone,* Someone living, Someone very near, Someone who shares my thoughts, my anxieties, my projects, Someone with whom I count, Someone on whom I can depend?

4. The world in which our pupils live is saturated with materialism. Today for the most part only that matters which can be seen, which can be touched, which can be felt. Am I careful to tell my pupils about the invisible world?

5. Do I understand thoroughly the realities that are unseen: God, the soul, divine life? Are they more real than the material things which are visible? The latter pass away, the former will never perish!

6. Do I know how to discover God in nature, a book which reveals the Creator, which reflects His beauty, His intelligence, His perfections, which is a subject for praise, a component part of expiation or of redemption?

7. Do I know how to recognize God in happenings which are disconcerting sometimes for our poor human logic? "My ways are not your ways," said Our

Lord. But, according to a Portuguese proverb: "God writes straight with crooked lines."

8. Do I know how to recognize God in other people? This is the surest foundation of charity.

Have I the habit of seeing souls in the faces of my pupils, and beyond those souls do I see Christ, who wishes to live in them and to grow in them?

Misserey wrote:

Creatures are only veils; pure eyes, loving eyes, pierce through the veils without being hindered by a thousand obstacles and go directly to the divine, hidden Reality. I cannot be at the foot of the altar always, O Jesus, but I can be continually near Your tabernacles of flesh . . .

When one enters a church, sometimes one must search a long time before finding the inner chapel where Jesus is hidden in His Sacrament of Love. A little lamp indicates the blessed spot, and we prostrate ourselves lovingly before the tabernacle which encloses the Sacred Host.

Men also enclose Jesus within themselves as in an immense, gloomy cathedral; often in such souls He is finally found after we have sought Him patiently; the feeble light in such souls indicates His presence so unsteadily! But He is there, unquestionably: Let us adore Him, let us serve Him lovingly. *Creatures are tabernacles of Jesus.* Alas, sometimes they are tabernacles without the Divine Host. But Jesus has been there. Jesus wants to return there; let us help Him to regain admission . . .

. . . My Jesus, make me understand these things fully; grant that at the same time I so love to prostrate myself before marble tabernacles which contain You in the Holy Eucharist, I may lovingly bend before those living tabernacles which are around me everywhere, and which really contain You! [4]

9. Have I understood thoroughly that my attitude at prayer time, my manner of making the Sign of the Cross, the glance of faith which I focus on the tabernacle have, quite unknown to me, more influence on souls than the most beautiful discourses? Faith is essentially contagious, but only if it is a complete faith, a loyal faith. Young people today have a prodigious capacity for discerning whatever is not genuine in Christian living.

10. Do I, by my accent when I speak, and especially by my consequent manner of acting, do I give others the conviction that I would be willing to shed my blood for the truths of my religion? "I have faith in those witnesses who are willing to be victims," said Pascal.

11. The best way to awaken and to strengthen faith in these dear young souls is to prove to them by my life that I believe truly all that I say.
Is my habitual deportment conformable to my teaching and to my words of advice? "They talk but do nothing," said our Lord of the Pharisees (Matt. 23:3). For an educator is there not a subtle danger of Pharisaism?

12. Have I understood that it is not sufficient to have a theoretical faith, but that one must cultivate the spirit of faith, that is to say: reflexes which make us act in conformity with supernatural realities in all circumstances? The ideal would be to live very naturally in the supernatural.

13. When acting do I have the sense of a hierarchy of values? Am I not inclined to judge things from my point of view rather than from God's point of view?

14. What is the general tendency of my preoccupations? What is the trend of my thoughts, of my conversations? Do I live habitually in interior conversation with God?

15. Is my motive of acting before all and above all the desire that God reign in all souls?

16. Would it not be well to purify my intentions more and more frequently? Is my heart disengaged from all self-seeking? *Where your treasure is there is your heart also.* Am I the center of my thoughts, or is Christ truly my treasure, my "chief concern," toward whom all that is in me is oriented?

Resolutions

1. Not to let a day pass without begging God, for myself and for the souls in my charge, an increase of faith. "Lord, I believe, but increase my faith!"

2. It is not enough to ask the grace of faith, it must be nourished. Nothing nourishes faith as does the word of God. To have a true devotion to Holy Scripture. To make myself a personal anthology of the inspired words. Not to fear to learn many by heart, to cite them often, but, above all, to live them.

3. Faith is a gift of God. It is a talent which we must cultivate so that it will bear fruit. By exercising it often one gives it strength.

4. To maintain a complete loyalty to what my faith requires, and for that reason to guard my actions and my affections. We are apt to be deluded! We are so tenacious of what we have, however little it may be, and as a result a screen or a mist hides God from us. But if we break away from whatever our consciences tell us is a barrier between our souls and God, the horizon clears and God lets us see Him anew.

5. To be watchful to banish all pride from our souls. Humility is necessary for the increase of faith. "We can know God only by acknowledging our faults. So those who have known God without recognizing their misery have not glorified Him, but themselves," said Pascal.

6. Not to be astonished if one has occasional temptations against faith. At such crises, to keep calm, to increase our humility and our petitions: "Lord, grant that I may see . . ." "Lord, I do believe, increase my faith." To act as if the temptation did not exist. "One must give oneself fully to the truth so that Truth may be given to him," Père Sertillanges used to love to repeat. Faith is a risk, but it is the most beautiful of risks, a risk that compensates.

Submission to God is one of the greatest acts of homage we can render to His Truth and to His love. Ste Thérèse wrote:

Whenever I find myself faced with the prospect of an attack by my enemy I am most courageous; I turn my back on him, without so much as looking at him, and run to

Jesus. I tell Him I am ready to shed all my blood to prove my faith in Heaven. I tell Him I am quite happy that the eyes of my soul should be blind, while I am on earth, to the heavenly wonders in store for me, so long as He will open the eyes of unbelieving souls for all eternity. . . .

. . . He whose Heart is ever watchful taught me that He works miracles even for those whose faith is like a tiny mustard seed, to make it grow, while, as in the case of His Mother, He works miracles for His dearest friends only after He has tested their faith. He let Lazarus die, even though Martha and Mary had sent word that he was sick; and when He was asked by our Lady at the marriage feast of Cana to help the master of the house, He said His time had not yet come. But after the trial, what rewards! Lazarus rises from the dead, and water becomes wine.[5]

7. Humility does not forbid courage; indeed, quite the contrary. We must not fear to have a courageous faith, above all at the hour of prayer.

Are you familiar with a famous episode in the life of M. Dupont, the "Holy Man of Tours"?

One day a young girl from Notre-Dame-la-Riche, having a sore foot that she had bruised and which had swelled enormously, was brought to the home of M. Dupont. He was at prayer. The young girl explained that she desired to visit the Shrine of the Holy Face so that she might tell God that "if it was His good pleasure and His will, she might be cured."

M. Dupont replied quietly: "That is not the way to pray . . . You have no faith! Tell God in a firm manner: Lord, cure me! . . . If you want to be cured you must command the good God!"

"Oh! that is too bold," replied the invalid. "I cannot command God!"

"Well! you have no faith," replied M. Dupont. "You must say: I want to be cured. Cure me. . . . One must pray with boundless confidence and not hesitate."

"O my God, it seems to me as if I do have faith," said the poor young girl.

Stirred to greater effort, she began to pray again. She could feel some improvement then, and she returned home on foot, although with difficulty. Encouraged by this unexpected favor and reproaching herself for her little faith, she said: "My God, it is true; I have doubted Your power and Your goodness in my regard. . . . I know that You can and that You want to heal me; I implore this grace. Give it to me, Lord, give it to me!"

She returned to M. Dupont and came home completely cured. The "Man of God" knew how to stir up her faith in spite of herself, a faith of which our Lord had said: "Amen, I say to you, whatsoever you ask with faith it will be done unto you."

PRAYER

Lord Jesus, who have said: "If you had faith even as small as a mustard seed, you could move mountains," give me that courageous faith which will enable me to conquer all obstacles, that I may find You in everything and everything in You. Have pity on the souls who are seeking You but who are still far from You. Have mercy on souls in doubt and who do not know how to find You. Have pity also, O Lord, on all those who seek You no more and who go through life without knowing whither they go. Multiply vocations in souls who have a burning and radiant faith. Make more and more efficacious the testimony of lives consecrated forever to Your love, that Your truth may be the better known.

AMEN

CHAPTER II

Silence, Our Strength

The modern world obliges men to live a feverish life and to labor intensely. The breathless tempo of the cities ends by wearing down the most placid temperaments. Religious souls, who though not *of* the world live *in* the world, realize that their religious life is influenced by the world.

Modern life with its accelerated tempo is never satisfied. It is supremely distracted by stage performances, by music records with their shameless dominance of noise, not to mention the shrieking of sirens, the bellowing of horns, the telephone bells, and the roaring of automobiles. In the end all of these combine to wear down the most solid nerves.

That explains the neuroses that we notice more and more in the young people under our care. That explains, also, particularly in metropolitan areas, the superficiality of souls and the need of combating it under all its forms.

Without any pessimism, one can say that there is truly a malady of the soul produced by this age of noise, a malady which is aggravated in certain homes where the radio and the television operate perpetually.

In this world which we must love as we find it so that we may help it to become what it should be, consecrated souls have a mission to create oases of silence and of peace. Hence the importance of closed retreats and days of recollection. Hence the importance of living a more solid interior life. Hence the importance, finally, of the example religious souls must give by the radiation of their silence penetrated by contemplation.

Are these not reasons, then, which should urge us to focus our prayer and our meditation on the strength which the grace of silence brings to our spiritual and apostolic life?

Today, more than ever, the word of Isaias is true for us: "In silence and in hope shall your strength be" (Isai. 30:15).

Meditation

"The silence of infinite spaces frightens me," wrote Pascal. Try, for a few moments, to withdraw from the noise surrounding us and from our current occupations, but without being frightened by the silence of the infinite.

Silence is the normal attitude of man as he faces the supernatural.

Let us ask God humbly to introduce us Himself into the intimacy of His silence.

According to the dispositions of our souls, we shall be able either to remain in peaceful quiet before the Lord, letting ourselves be imbued with His Presence, or we shall begin immediately a colloquy of detached phrases which will lead us finally to be absorbed by His word.

If we prefer it, we can here make use of the ideas in the meditation which follows; they will convince us more and more of the reasons which should urge us to a love of silence.

The examen of conscience and the resolutions will help us to determine the efforts we will make, according to the state of our soul, and according to our circumstances.

Silence, a requisite for finding God and for making our actions more fruitful.

Silence facilitates our meeting with God. It is true that we can find God everywhere, even in the midst of a crowd. But the Lord Jesus, who knows so thoroughly the laws of human psychology, recommends silence and solitude. "When thou prayest, go into thy room, and closing thy door, pray to thy Father in secret; and thy Father, who sees in secret, will reward thee" (Matt. 6:6).

St. John of the Cross wrote:

"The Heavenly Father has spoken but one Word: that is His Son, the Word made flesh. He speaks It eternally and in an eternal silence. It is in the silence of the soul that that Word is heard."

It is in silence that the eternal generation of the Word and the inspiration of the Holy Spirit are accomplished. It is in silence that the effectual workings of grace take place in the soul; so, too, the participation in the divine life. It is in silence that God communicates life to our organism. It is in silence that the sap rises, that the tree buds forth and bears fruit. Silence is the great law of life.

Fleeing from the anger of Jezebel and strengthened by the bread provided by the angel, the Prophet had walked forty days in the desert and had come to Horeb, the Mountain of God, where Yahweh had appeared to Moses many times.

And he said to him: Go forth, and stand upon the mount before the Lord. And behold the Lord passeth. And a great and strong wind before the Lord overthrowing the mountains, and breaking the rocks in pieces: the Lord is not in the wind. And after the wind an earthquake: the Lord is not in the earthquake. And after the earthquake a fire: the Lord is not in the fire. And after the fire a whistling of a gentle air. And when Elias heard it, he covered his face with his mantle, and coming forth stood in the entering in of the cave. . . . (3 Kings 19:11–13)

The Lord was in the soft murmur of the gentle breeze.

"The soul must find silence again so that God may be revealed to it and communicate with it." God speaks to every soul. If there are those who do not hear Him, it is because they do not listen. In the Apocalypse (3:20), He compares Himself to the Friend who knocks at the door. One must listen to His voice so that He may enter and reveal His intimate secrets.

Let us read again the episode of Martha and Mary:

Now it came to pass as they were on their journey, that he entered a certain village; and a woman named Martha welcomed him to her house. And she had a sister called Mary, who also seated herself at the Lord's feet, and listened to his word. But Martha was busy about much serving. She came up and said, "Lord, is it no concern of thine that my sister has left me to serve alone? Tell her therefore to help me." But the Lord answered and said to her, "Martha, Martha, thou art anxious and troubled about many things; and yet only one thing is needful. Mary has chosen the best part, and it will not be taken away from her" (Luke 10:38–42).

Most certainly Jesus appreciates our work . . . He is waiting for our repentance . . . He loves our prayer . . . But He judges our love by the manner in which we listen to Him.

Let us note that silence, that it may not defeat its purpose, requires some respite. Relaxation at recreations is part of the asceticism of silence. "Whoever wants to make an angel, makes a beast," said Pascal. And St. Teresa of Avila did not hesitate to take over the organization of the community recreations and to lead the happy chorus of her daughters with the help of castanets or of a tambourine. Nor did she hesitate one day to reprimand a Sister whose ill-timed devotion had made her prefer prayer to a community recreation. Everything is to be according to proportion, to equilibrium and . . . to charity. It is no less true that zones and hours of silence are indispensable for fruitful action as for contemplation.

"Silence is the surest guardian of the religious spirit," said St. Basil.

Silence, a definite need for the soul which desires to amend and to be "reformed."

He who continually gives himself without renewing his resources ends by emptying himself.

The obligations of the active life strain not only the muscles of the body, but the energies of the soul as well. The return to silence is a physical and a moral condition for relaxation and for reorienting oneself.

In a life of action the immediate and absorbing task hides the total view of life, as a tree hides the forest. One must know how to judge calmly the action that is of the past and to plan for future activity.

Noise scatters, squanders, and confuses. Silence gathers, retrieves, and condenses. He who does not arrange for zones of silence is hastening the time when he will live on the surface of his soul.

Talkativeness is extremely harmful to the spiritual life and to fruitful action. A prattler has no time, and soon has no relish, for recollection, for thinking, for living seriously. Moreover, by the agitation he creates around him he prevents others from doing their work and from being recollected. Superficial and vain as he is, the chatterer is a dangerous creature.

It is silence which gives depth to the words which we speak.

Maurice Maeterlinck wrote: "Souls are weighed in silence as gold or silver are weighed in pure water. The words we speak have sense only because of the silence wherein they bathe." [1]

Souls for whom silence is a burden are those whose hold on spirituality is very weak. The more a soul has received in silence, the more she has to give out in action.

Silence, a duty of humility, of justice, and of charity.

There are many aspects of humility. That which shows our nothingness and displays our unworthiness is one of them. But there is another, perhaps more important: that which advises us not to speak of oneself so that one may forget oneself and think rather of God and of our neighbor.

Nothing is more vain than to talk of oneself, either to say something good or bad.

The humility of Mary shines out in her Magnificat when she proclaims the lowliness of the handmaid of the Lord. It shines, too, in her silence when she returns from Hebron, waiting until God Himself, by His angel, will assuage the anguish of Joseph.

Robert de Langeac wrote:

We must seek to please God so that He may look down on us with ever-increasing pleasure, instead of thinking out ways and means of constantly impressing others, pressing into service not only our natural gifts, but even our supernatural graces. Such spiritual vanity is the worst of all and is a certain sign that what we parade is not a real grace, or at least that God will cease to grant us such graces. It is not thus that one enters His kingdom.[2]

There are some secrets of the King we must guard jealously, as there are also secrets of souls that we must respect very carefully. A religious receives many confidences, and her experience enables her to guess many things. The secrets of others do not belong to us. Silence is for us a duty of elementary justice.

As Seneca said: "Tell no one what you want no one to know. If you are not master of yourself, how can you count on the silence of others?"

There is nothing more dangerous for the peace of a consecrated soul, for union of hearts in a community, for the blessing of God on an apostolic work, than the spirit of criticism.

The spirit of criticism is a poison, a never-dying worm, a cancer in a healthy organism. It absorbs the vital energies of the one who criticizes, of the one who listens to the criticism, and of those who are criticized. The spirit of criticism is the spirit of Satan.

To judge is to usurp a right which belongs to God alone. By what right do we judge? God alone can judge, for He alone knows the proportion of the graces received and of the graces neglected by each soul.

For in many things we all offend. If anyone does not

offend in word, he is a perfect man, able also to lead around by a bridle the whole body. For if we put bits into horses' mouths that they may obey us, we control their whole body also. Behold, even the ships, great as they are, and driven by boisterous winds, are steered by a small rudder wherever the touch of the steersman pleases. So the tongue also is a little member, but it boasts mightily. Behold, how small a fire—how great a forest it kindles! And the tongue is a fire, the very world of iniquity. . . . Every kind of beast and bird, and of serpents and the rest, is tamed and has been tamed by mankind; but the tongue no man can tame—a restless evil, full of deadly poison. With it we bless God the Father; and with it we curse men, who have been made after the likeness of God. . . . These things, my brethren, ought not to be so. (James 3:2-11)

Colloquy

My daughter, come near to Me, and let Me first envelop you in silence. . . .

You need to recover calmness. For a few minutes let all the distractions of the world be deadened in you.

You need to recover peace. For a little while try to think neither of yourself nor of your work.

You need to find Me again in order to be refreshed, in order that you may be grounded again in the truth, that you may be renewed in My love. Forget all except Me. Be willing to forget yourself. Think that I am there with you, that I look upon you, that I love you.

It is hard to stop thinking of self. I understand. But it is a renunciation which pays.

Concentrate on My Presence. I am there with you . . . I am looking upon you . . . I love you . . .

Silence is My law. Silence is My sphere. Silence is My atmosphere.

From all eternity a current of intense life passes from My Father to Me, and from Me to My Father.

From all eternity the Holy Spirit proceeds from Our contemplation, from Our praise, from Our Love.

In silence the Father begot Me; in silence I praise the Father.

In silence the Holy Spirit proceeds from Our mutual love.

It is in silence that Our intimate life is enjoyed, is expressed, rejoices: the silence of the Infinite!

In silence also My Love is revealed to a soul. In silence you will be able to understand the beatings of My heart.

I have loved silence so much.

In silence I became Incarnate; in silence I was born, far from the cities, far from noise, in the silence of midnight.

I spent the greater part of My earthly life in silence. When the hour came for Me to preach, I began by a forty days' retreat in the desert. I interrupted My ministry by numerous periods of silence by night and by day.

During the Passion, instead of defending Myself, I was silent. And in the Sacred Host, I continue to be the Great Silent One.

My daughter, who can tell how much evil has been brought to your soul by sterile restlessness? Surely there is a time to speak and a time to be silent. When I send you to work for souls, you should keep united with Me, at least in desire. Your word is barren if I do not speak it.

Your activity is nothing, your devotedness is nothing if I do not fructify it.

He who does not gather with Me, scatters. He who seeks himself, believing that he works for Me, works but in vain.

That is why it is necessary from time to time to take "baths" of silence, as it were, wherein you can silence the discordant voices of pride and of egotism; wherein you can empty all the hidden pockets of bitterness or of hatred; above all, wherein you can listen to My voice speaking within you, to My voice which calms, to My voice which purifies, to My voice which unifies.

Then, in the time of action, throughout your activity, it is I who act. When you think of your poor people, you think of Me. When you live for your children, you live for Me. When you nurse your sick ones, you nurse Me. When you serve your Sisters, you serve Me. And I supply for your insufficiency, I repair your errors, I give full value to the least of your movements.

My daughter, it is the love of silence which leads Me to the silence of love.

Silence is not God. The Word is God. But it is in silence that the Father speaks the Word, and that the Word operates. Most often it is without noise of words that the Uncreated Word makes Himself heard by His creature. According as the creature is disposed to listen, according as his heart is detached from creatures, will his soul be truly receptive.

The heart has a language the lips know not. Two people who love each other deeply have no need of poor human words to profess their love. The silence of love is more eloquent than any amount of prattling, especially when one of the two concerned is God, who is love Itself.

My daughter, do not forget this: it is in the intimate silence of consecrated souls that the destinies of the world are at stake.

What a pity when souls, burdened with trifles, are void of the one thing necessary!

In spite of their frequently tragic character, the events of history are only a cropping out of an underlying drama: that of the struggle between love and indifference (when it is not actually hatred) within hearts, that of the struggle between generosity and meanness in human wills.

It is from within that the world is lost. Likewise it is from within that the world is saved. You have been chosen from thousands of others to consecrate your strength to the salvation of your spiritual sons and daughters, so that in them the Father may be glorified! It is in silence from within that take place the mysterious childbirths of the communion of saints.

It is in silence and from within that you nourish your spiritual children as a mother nourishes the child that she carries in her womb.

It is in silence and from within that you expiate their faults and that you provide them with the helps they need most.

It is in silence, My daughter, that you will find peace, that you will find quiet, that you will find strength, that you will find fruitfulness; because in silence you will find your Saviour and your God.

Examen

1. In my life do I have times of silence sufficient to soothe my nerves, to readjust myself, and above all, to find God again?

2. Have I not noticed that, when I permit feverish activity to dominate me, then I fail more easily in charity?

3. Am I faithful to all the practices of the religious life, all of which have as their purpose to insure an atmosphere of silence? In community: doors closed gently, a minimum of noise in the corridors, a moderate tone of voice, a scrupulous respect for the sacred silence at the time and in the places recommended by the Rule.

4. Have I understood that if silence is a favorable method for finding God, it is essentially the act of faith in the Divine Presence which gives to silence its true meaning and all its efficacy?

5. To facilitate interior silence, do I remain faithful while permitting myself legitimate exceptions without scruple; while respecting the elementary rules of charity, am I faithful to avoid all giddiness by indiscreet glances, by useless curiosity, by superfluous chattering, by idle reading?

6. In the discharge of her duties a religious often hears confidences or secrets. Am I scrupulously faithful to all the rules regarding the professional secret?

7. Have I understood that silence is often a safeguard against failings in charity and in humility? Nothing

scandalizes a soul more than to hear from consecrated lips words of disparagement or of vanity.

8. Have I been duly impressed with the fact that silence, which is a precious power, can become under certain circumstances a dangerous weakness when it is simply the expression of ill humor, of wounded pride, or of laxity (for example, if there is question of defending the honor of God, or of a reputation threatened)?

Resolutions

1. To safeguard, at any price, as a treasure and for the greater good of souls, the times of recollection and of silence prescribed by my holy Rule.

2. When I feel myself burdened by overactivity, I will stop courageously, if only for a few seconds, to renew contact with the interior Guest of my soul.

3. To organize most carefully my work and my time. The examen twice a day, with the careful arrangement of duties, enables us more easily to keep our serenity, and to face calmly the unexpected.

4. Never to give myself over to a feverish activity which makes me lose control of myself. If I do so, I shall make it known to my superior and to my director.

5. If silence weighs upon me at certain hours, I shall offer it to God to expiate my failings in silence, and to repair my faults against charity.

6. To create around me a calm, silent atmosphere. To avoid useless movements and useless words. To mod-

erate the tone of my voice. Children, particularly, are impressed by a gentle, modulated voice rather than by strident tones or repeated corrections.

7. As much as possible to avoid speaking of myself. To avoid speaking particularly of positions I have held or projects that I have completed. Any comparison with my former assignments runs the risk of being interpreted unfavorably.

8. Never to impose silence on children as a punishment, but as an honor. Only souls that are masters of themselves can keep silence.

9. Not to oblige children to keep silence too long. To take into consideration their ages, their temperaments, and the requirements of a particular situation.

10. To practice silence and to give them a relish for it, one should teach children educative games designed for the purpose.

11. Before entering a church or a hall where silence is required, to pause a little to become recollected.

12. Before prayer to ask the children themselves to take a recollected attitude: by walking on tiptoe, for example, and by avoiding noise with chairs or benches.

13. During services, to speak in a whisper, in a few words. To assume a recollected attitude. To create an atmosphere of recollection and of the supernatural. Whoever leads children in prayer should make use of times of silence to guide their intentions discreetly; for example, to suggest to them to repeat softly a sentence which they have said in a loud tone.

PRAYER

Holy Virgin Mary, model of contemplative souls, teach us how to keep recollected in the midst of the distractions of active life. Shield us not only from the feverishness of activity, but from the subtle recoiling of egotism. Obtain for us that the noise of passing things may not make us forget the silent presence of Him who dwells within us. That the fascination of visible things may not turn our hearts from the hidden splendors of the invisible world, develop in us a relish for silence. Teach us, after your example, to make our active apostolate a faithful communion with the will of the Father for the humble service of Jesus in our souls.

AMEN

CHAPTER III

Uprightness and Loyalty

Why is it that evil tongues can say: "Sometimes there is more honesty among lay people than among religious"? Is the abuse of the *distinguo* and of mental reservations the cause of such a statement? May this not originate possibly in the fact that some people, through laudable anxiety, badly expressed, strive to safeguard discretion, charity, and prudence?

To the young people of today all this seems very much complicated.

Would it not seem necessary to return to the simplicity of the Gospel, a simplicity which does not exclude wisdom, but for which "yes" is yes, "no" is no, a simplicity which is not entangled with ambiguous formulae?

Our young people thirst after sincerity, and they declare willingly—sometimes violently—their reactions against all conformism. But are they themselves always exempt from that virus of deceit which is infiltrated into their thoughts and into their lives in an imperceptible way?

If they are so exacting with others, are they themselves loyal to God always, loyal to themselves, loyal to all legitimate authority?

Intelligent cultivation of loyalty must be one of the major concerns of every educator. But let us not forget that the fundamental element of this cultivation is the unquestionable testimony that each educator must give of the complete uprightness of her own life.

As in all else, it is from the Master of all truth that we shall learn the secret of all this; it is from Him that we shall receive the strength for this.

Meditation

Let us begin by adoring the Lord Jesus as He declares: "I am the Truth" (John 14:6); "I have come into the world to bear witness to the Truth" (John 18:37); "I hate a mouth with a double tongue" (Prov. 8:13); "The Truth shall make you free" (John 8:32).

Let us see with what severity He scourges liars and hypocrites. For that reason let us read again the twenty-third chapter of St. Matthew:

The Scribes and Pharisees have sat on the chair of Moses. All things, therefore, that they command you, observe and do. But do not act according to their works; for they talk but do nothing. And they bind together heavy and oppressive burdens, and lay them on men's shoulders; but not with one finger of their own do they choose to move them. In fact, all their works they do in order to be seen by men. . . . They love the first places . . . and greetings. . . . But woe to you, Scribes and Pharisees, hypocrites! (2–13)

Here follow the celebrated curses: *blind guides . . . the unclean dishes . . . whited sepulchres, which outwardly seem to men beautiful, but within are full of dead men's bones and of all uncleanness.*

The definition which St. John has given of the Word Incarnate is contained in these few words: "In him is the fullness of grace and of truth" (1:14).

First and foremost Jesus asked of His disciples a complete loyalty. When He saw Nathaniel approaching Him, He said: "Behold a true Israelite in whom there is no guile" (John 1:47).

Nothing disheartens Him more than tepidity, fruit of complacent self-delusion.

This is what is said in the Apocalypse of the Church at Laodicea: "I know thy works; thou art neither cold nor hot. But because thou art lukewarm . . . I am about to vomit thee out of my mouth; because thou sayest, 'I am rich . . .' and dost not know that thou art the wretched and miserable and poor and blind and naked one. I counsel thee to anoint thy eyes with eye salve that thou mayest see" (3:14–18).

Let us tell Jesus again our desire that there be in our consciences no hidden fold, no obscure corner. May He deign to make us as transparent as the crystal so that He may penetrate us completely with His divine light.

Let us open our souls and our hearts completely to the rays of the divine Sun, and remain thus, silently, under the influence of those rays.

"And the Light shines in the darkness" (John 1:5).

In order to sharpen our thirst for truth, let us use the following thoughts. There is no question of reading them rapidly, all at once, but of assimilating them slowly, then of having them evolve in ardent prayer, adapting them to the needs of our souls.

"We are all more or less in disguise," wrote Father Faber. "Perfect uprightness of soul is an exceptional grace. The first step toward sincerity is to be conscious that we are very far from it."

"Every man is a liar," says Holy Scripture (Ps. 115: 11). Who, then, can swear that he is perfectly sincere? Who can flatter himself that he is genuinely true?

There is nothing that God hates more than a lie. Satan is the father of lies. There is nothing that God loves more than the truth, for He is Truth itself.

There is nothing that God desires to grant to us more than loyalty, for in Him there is no evasion. There is nothing that men forget to pray for more than uprightness, for no one is willing to admit that he lacks it.

The most terrible punishment of the soul which, more or less consciously, seeks to deceive others, is to end by being deceived itself.

One may be deceived himself; one may deceive men; one does not deceive God. A day will come when the masks will fall, when one will be seen as one is, in all truth, with the eye of Him who sees us as we truly are.

The best way of being shrewd with God, with others, with oneself, is to be honest.

The arguments which the Apostles used in asking uprightness and loyalty of the first Christians were not drawn from sociological comparisons, but from a reference to God and to the Mystical Body: "You have been created to the image of God, that is why you renounce falsehood," said St. Paul. "Wherefore, put away lying and speak truth each one with his neighbor, because we are members of one another" (Eph. 4:25).

"Lay aside therefore all malice, and all deceit, and pretense, and envy, and all slander" (1 Pet. 2:1).

Only loyal souls can hear the voice of the Master

within them: "Everyone who is of the truth hears my voice" (John 18:37).

Fidelity to truth, in all charity, is the *sine qua non* for spiritual growth: "Rather are we to practise the truth in love, and so grow up in all things in Christ" (Eph. 4:15).

Thomas à Kempis wrote: "If all were right with you, and you were well purified from sin, everything would tend to your good and your profit." [1]

"A truth which is not charitable proceeds from a charity which is not true," St. Francis de Sales used to say.

Here is one point in spiritual uprightness: at the hour of prayer, to give our whole hearts to the words we pronounce. Often the lips speak but the soul is silent.

"The Lord is nigh unto all them that call upon him: to all that call upon him in truth" (Ps. 144:18).

In the spiritual notes of Estelle Fagette, of Pellevoisin, one finds, under the date of February 11, 1876, the following words, as if spoken by our Lady:

If you wish to serve me, be simple, and let your words and actions agree. What afflicts me most is the lack of respect shown to my Son in Holy Communion, and the attitude, the pious attitude, taken at prayer when the mind is busy about other things. I say this for persons who pretend to be pious.

Humility is a help to loyalty, for very often it is pride that creates mirages for us. On the other hand, honesty makes us humble: "For if anyone thinks himself to be something, whereas he is nothing, he deceives himself" (Gal. 6:3).

Loyalty is not brutality. Our Lord did not hesitate to

say to His apostles: "Many things yet I have to say to you, but you cannot bear them now" (John 16:12).

There are some lights that are too hard on weak eyes. There is no question of dazzling at the risk of blinding. One must take into account the possibilities of receptivity of those who have a right to know the truth. In some cases the disclosure must be progressive, must be sifted carefully; but at all times we should be sure that our light is authentic, so that our souls may be sincere and our hearts loyal.

Colloquy

Meditation is addressed to the intellect more directly in order to train it to reflect and to ponder the various aspects of a spiritual problem. But the most important part of a contemplation is the colloquy.

"Prayer," said St. Teresa of Avila, "is a heart-to-heart talk with the Host adored in our souls and in our tabernacles." This definition implies something more than a pious reading of a meditation, more even than a more or less speculative reflection, more than a monologue in which the soul talks continually. It is rather, after the manner of Mary Magdalene, a fervent attention of the soul to the words, to the sentiments, to the ideas of the Master.

The art of hearing and of listening to our Lord so as to live more closely to Him, that is the whole art of prayer and of true wisdom. As Thomas à Kempis wrote:

"I will hear what the Lord God speaks within me" (Ps. 84:9). Blessed is the soul that hears the Lord speaking within her, and receives from His mouth the word of consolation.

Blessed the ears that catch the pulses of the divine whisper (Job 4:12), and take no notice of the whisperings of this world.[2]

The author of the *Imitation* does not hesitate on another count (is it literary procedure, is it pious fiction? Would it not rather be because of ideas awakened in him by union with his divine Master?), he does not hesitate, I say, to outline the scheme of interior conversation, timidly, at first, then in his third book giving more and more place to the voice of Christ speaking to His disciple. Is not that point one of the charms, one of the reasons for the efficacious unction of this admirable book, which has helped so many generations of Christians and of religious to enter more intimately into union with Christ?

"My Beloved to me and I to Him." The colloquy has for a climax what the Sulpician method of prayer calls the communion, and which is, fundamentally, nothing else than a mystical embrace of the soul and its God, where, by a mutual gift, there operates in the soul a most complete saturation of the virtues of Christ.

It is evident that in the colloquy above all, nothing can take the place of personal conversation; the words of the colloquy have no other end than to attract the soul to this mysterious and admirable exchange which must be the rule in the relations of Jesus with the consecrated soul.

My daughter, I am the truth. Truth is My name as much as charity. Truth and charity, as well as justice and love, are poor human words that express as well as they can but without compelling force to define them fully, the various aspects of the divine transcendence.

My daughter, there is nothing that horrifies Me more than duplicity in a consecrated soul. I thirst for uprightness and simplicity.

I know your weakness. I am ready to pardon every weakness. But what I do want to find in you is a sound will and complete loyalty.

If you but knew how the lack of sincerity paralyzes souls! Why are they unwilling to admit to themselves their true intentions? Are they afraid of Me? Do they not believe that I read them through and through?

Come to Me, then, such as you are, without dissimulation, without disguise. Bring Me your misery and I will cure you. Do not try to deceive Me. You do yourself harm by wishing to hide from Me the toxins which are poisoning you.

As if I did not know you! As if I did not want to save you!

Take care! During My public life I intervened only for the unfortunate who showed Me their wounds and who, by themselves or through their neighbors, called on Me for help.

There is nothing more dangerous than to live in self-deception. You have comparatively only a little time to spend here on earth. Think often of Me; consider My manner of seeing people, things, events, and above all, yourself. That is the secret of true knowledge and of fundamental wisdom.

You can never meditate too much on My words: "Seek ye first the Kingdom of God and His justice; all the rest will be added unto you." How do you think that I can bless your life, your work, your speech when the most elementary justice is not respected?

Be loyal in your charity. Do not be content to show kindness to a soul whom, in the depths of your heart, you do not esteem. Put your kindness to work to seek and to find the beauty hidden in that soul whom you are not inclined to like.

Be careful to live your life in accord with what you believe. You believe in My presence? You believe in My love? You believe in My power? Then . . . ?

You believe that I am in you, and you in Me? You believe that I am the only one who counts: that is to say, what I am, what I think, what I desire, what I expect?

You believe that I am hidden in all souls and that I consider as done to Me the good or evil that you mete out to them?

Then . . . ? After all that, judge your own conduct.

My daughter, sermons are not what lead people back to the Church after they have abandoned Me. What brings them back? The actions of the children of Holy Mother Church, and primarily of the consecrated members of the Church.

Consecrated souls, you are responsible for those souls whom you deprive of truth when you scandalize them by your unreasonable actions, by your thoughtlessness.

Have a love for truth. Where truth reigns, I reign. Many of your meannesses which now blind you would disappear of themselves if you would renounce your own judgment, your own opinion, your self-love, to consider My judgment, My opinion, My love. For, fundamentally, one must always come back to this: to renounce yourself, finite as you are; to unite yourself with Me, the Infinite.

With Me everything is enlightened, everything is enlarged, everything is simplified, everything is solved, everything is transfigured.

With Me, everything becomes beautiful, because everything tends toward the truth.

Why do you seek your satisfaction in yourself or in the esteem of others? Have you not experienced yet how winds change, how human opinions vary?

Praises, glory, publicity, reputation? Mere smoke from a fire in some dead leaves!

Do not let yourself be seduced by what is only on the surface, by what is passing. When will you ever understand the hierarchy of true values? Why do you seek yourself in the action that you declare you are performing only for My Glory? Why are you so sensitive still about what one thinks of you, and about what is said of you? All is vain that is not truly in Me or for Me!

Beyond appearances, I look for truth in the depths of hearts. What counts in My eyes is the interior effort, the hidden generosity, the upright intention.

Visible results depend upon Me more than upon you. They can have their usefulness, their reason for existence, but for a limited time only. What is more important is that they are your honest decisions. That is where your free will works for or against love. Choice and upright intentions are what have an eternal influence.

My daughter, the love that is the test of truth is that

love which forbids all craftiness, all dissimulation in your dealings with your Sisters and with your Superiors.

If you must exaggerate, let it be in an upright way (without ever wounding charity); I shall not reproach you for it. And you will make reparation for so many distorted consciences!

My kindness and My indulgence are immense. If you could see the extent of them, you would be overwhelmed, for your limited notions of justice would be completely confused. But I am adamant with dishonest compromises. Light cannot unite with darkness; one or the other must disappear.

I hate duplicity which, unwilling to acknowledge its secret intentions, covers them with a mask of virtue. To the soul which consents to its lure it brings the worst of chastisements: blindness of soul.

The greatest crimes are those committed against My Spirit, for they check life at its very source. Guard against all deceit!

As the sap passes from the trunk of the tree, so My grace passes freely into the religious soul united to its Superior. When this union is only apparent, it is as if the branch were attached to the trunk by the bark; the sap does not pass into it; nor does My grace go to a disloyal religious.

I do not like prayers that are merely recited forms. Say your prayers as if you were talking to Me. I prefer that you do not talk to Me rather than have to listen to you saying things that you do not think. Make your will agree with your words, or be silent. Formulae recited without your thought in them: that is not you, it means nothing to Me, for it is you that I want.

It will be at the hour of death that you will understand how much I have loved you in the truth. Profit by the time that is given to you before it is too late, in order to serve Me in the truth.

Examen

1. Have I been deeply concerned about my complete loyalty: to God . . . to myself . . . to my Superiors . . . to the souls confided to my care?

2. What is my habitual reaction when I witness deceit, dissimulation, injustice?

3. Have I a true horror of deceit under whatever form it appears? In others? In myself?

4. What are my specific reasons for hating deceit? Are they in the religious category, the moral, the educative?
   Do I really understand that God is truth and that Satan is a liar?

5. How does my vigilance to live in strict truthfulness show itself? In my examen of conscience? Analyze under the eyes of God, without scruple, but without indulgence. Is there honesty, without useless details, in my confessions? Am I completely open with my director? Do uprightness and simplicity govern my relations with our chaplain, with my superiors, with my associates, with my pupils?

6. Do I try, at community prayers, to concentrate my will on the formulae recited in the name of all the souls I represent?

7. Am I sufficiently persuaded that the least disloyalty on the part of an educator ruins her moral authority and opens the door to deformations of conscience?

8. Have I understood that if I must avoid personally as a plague every failing in loyalty or in justice, I must not be astonished if sometimes I am a victim of lying and even of calumny? Could I not accept this in order to repair my weaknesses, more or less conscious, in that regard, and help to expiate all the faults committed in the world against truth?

9. What is my attitude when I am accused falsely or when I am treated unjustly? Is it revolt, a groaning complaint, gloomy resignation, revengeful defense? Or rather, while searching as calmly as possible for means to re-establish the truth, do I commune with my Master calumniated in order to thank Him for giving me something to offer Him for the Redemption of the world?

Is it not normal that a consecrated soul should know by experience the bitterness of the Passion and bear some likeness to the Redeemer? But that she may not lose courage, the Lord who dwells within her is Himself her support and her strength. One day in Heaven, Truth will triumph, and she will see what all the present has availed, and she will wish that she had suffered more.

Resolutions

1. In spite of the fact that I have most sincere desires for a loyalty without equivocation, I must not believe too readily that I am exempt from self-delusion.
   To ask God daily for the grace of complete uprightness.

2. To put myself under the direction of the Holy Spirit, that I may think, act, and speak according to His light.

3. To be very faithful to the particular and general examinations of conscience, which are concerned not so much with exterior failings as with upright intentions.

4. To reject completely and with energy every trace of duplicity that is noticeable in me; and to share our Lord's horror of deceit and of hypocrisy.

5. At all times, especially with children, I must give an example of a scrupulous loyalty. Thus I must never promise or threaten what I cannot carry out moderately.

6. If one cannot reply frankly to an indiscreet or inopportune question of a child, not to fear to say to her: "I cannot reply to your question now, but I shall tell you later"; or else: "It is impossible for me to answer you, for that is a secret which I must keep"; but to avoid replying by a lie which sooner or later will be revealed. A child is never resigned to being deceived.

7. As a child is always inclined to imitate the life of

favorite heroes, one must be watchful to choose stories in which the principal character is irreproachable from the point of view of loyalty.

8. To explain sincerity as a condition of mutual confidence, as a mark of true courage.

9. To make children understand that even if one can deceive man, one cannot deceive God, who is a witness nothing escapes.

10. To dramatize biblical scenes which exalt honesty and punish dishonesty—for example, the story of Ananias and Sapphira (Acts 5:1–11).

11. To create an atmosphere of confidence in the classroom, mindful that the child taken into confidence lies less easily than one does in an atmosphere of suspicion.

12. To emphasize the fact that one who lies is, indeed, to be pitied, for he loses all right to confidence.

13. Never to give the child the impression that we expect him to lie. Avoid such announcements as this: "Above all, do not lie!" Say rather: "I am sure that you are going to tell me the truth." To believe a child capable of lying is to plant in her mind the idea of the possibility of lying.

14. Never to praise the intelligence of a child who has been able, shrewdly, but thanks to dishonesty, to get out of a scrape, or to deceive a comrade; that would be definite encouragement to repeat the offense.

15. To praise courageous honesty, whether the child be the author of it or the witness of it.

16. To grant the child the benefit of the doubt as long as one cannot verify his words; that raises him in his own estimation and gives him a higher idea of the virtue of honesty.

17. To brand the lie. To point out the baseness and the dishonesty of it each time that an occasion occurs.

18. To use foresight in pointing out the baseness of cheating and of trickery. Show how they are harmful to the general interest. For example, a game in which one cheats loses all its appeal; a composition which has been copied gives one a false rating.

19. Not to make honesty too difficult. Not to dramatize investigations. The teacher who proclaims with an angry air: "Let the one who has done this beware," and who then asks: "Are you the one?" frightens the culprit so that he will not confess.

20. If one perceives that a child has not told the truth, one should not be hasty in accusing him of a lie. Avoid hasty generalization: it is always to our interest, for the first time, to consider the dishonesty an apparent one, and to say to the child: "Oh, I know that you are honest, that you do not want to deceive me, but you have deceived yourself; the next time take care not to speak before you are sure of what you say."

21. To distinguish between objective and subjective untruth. There are some timid children who do not know how to express themselves; there are also some children who are more or less mythomaniacs, victims

of their imaginations. The true teacher seeks to analyze the real reason that has urged the child to lie: it may be fear, suggestion, vanity, self-interest, spitefulness; but it may also be a motive of charity to save a culprit. One readily sees that these lies are of different degrees of gravity.

22. If one sees that a child abuses confidence that has been given to her, tell her in a grieved tone that you must deprive her of such confidence for a certain time. Promise to reinstate her if, at the end of the time agreed upon, she has shown perfect honesty.

23. Teach the child to acquire tact; frankness does not consist in speaking of a private matter whenever one wishes, to whom one wishes.

PRAYER

Lord Jesus, who came into this world to give testimony to the truth, preserve us from every compromise with dishonesty or error, have pity on our weakness, and grant that we may never give the sad example of a discord between our faith and our life. Grant us such concern for the truth that in no circumstance shall we evade it. Help us to increase uprightness and loyalty in all the souls You confide to us, so that we may help them to rise toward You, the Light.

AMEN

CHAPTER IV

Our Royal Service

Today people no longer wish to serve. In fact, they do not know how to serve any more. Under the pretext of self-government, they make themselves a law unto themselves. Under the pretext of independence, they reject all constraint, however legitimate. Under the pretext of expansion they want to change all existing arrangements and to shatter all laws, even when the latter are an expression of an age-old tradition or are the products of normal conditions of development, conditions affecting the community and its citizens.

In reality, he who refuses to serve becomes a slave—a slave of his caprices, of his imagination, of his impulses, of public opinion, of customs, of the most volatile and contradictory trends sometimes. He becomes a slave also of his passions and of his instincts, sometimes of what is least desirable in his character.

On the other hand, the spirit of service understood in the Gospel sense is the source of true liberty and of inestimable enrichment.

How many times does the liturgy—in the Sunday collects, in the Office of Holy Saturday, in the Pontifical—recall this striking truth: "To serve God is to reign."

That is true because the characteristics of the one served are reflected in the server. That is true also because the service of the Lord—obedience to His Commandments and to His counsels, fidelity to the inspirations of grace—brings man back to his first destiny and makes him master of all animal life in nature and lord of all creation.

At this time when so many diverse doctrines tend toward abolition of disinterested self-sacrifice and of all moral law affecting exterior affairs, it is important to give young people again a deep reverence for the royal beauty of that little word: *to serve*. At the same time, we ourselves must try to understand better all of its hidden splendor.

Meditation

Let us adore Jesus prefigured in the Prophets under the title of "Servant of Yahweh."

When He came to this earth His first word was to express His role of servant: "Behold I come to do thy will, O God" (Heb. 10:9). He expressed it more definitely later: "The Son of Man also has not come to be served but to serve" (Mark 10:45).

Let us try, in the light of the Gospel, to share this spirit of service which is one of the dominant notes of our adored Master's psychology, a note which characterized His holy Mother, a note which He wishes to find in each of us who have the commission to help in the extension of His kingdom.

Even when the demon sums up his attitude by refusing to serve: *Non serviam,* the Word Incarnate, the King of Kings, Supreme Master of the Universe, proclaims His attitude by these words: *I am a servant.*

This will to serve is apparent throughout the Gospel.

When our Lady finds Him in the Temple, He explains His conduct by this decisive reason: the service of the Father (Luke 2:49).

How many times does He repeat: "I am in your midst as one who serves" (Luke 22:27); "I do always the things that are pleasing to Him" (John 8:29); "I seek not my own glory; there is one who seeks and who judges" (John 8:50).

In most of the parables He refers to the role of servant, and we can infer therefrom the qualities of service He expects from us:

. . . *Humble service:* imposing actions and words are not what count in His eyes.

. . . *Efficacious service:* He wishes from His servants actions more than words. "Not everyone who says to me, 'Lord, Lord,' shall enter the kingdom of heaven; but he who does the will of my father in heaven shall enter the kingdom of heaven" (Matt. 7:21).

. . . *Exact service:* always ready, always watchful. The Lord asks for an accounting when one least expects it.

. . . *Conscientious service:* One must be as faithful when the Lord seems far away as when He seems close.

. . . *Courageous service:* He praises the servant who recognized the value of the talents confided to him and blames severely the lazy servant who buried in the earth the sum he had received.

. . . *Disinterested service:* No one is indispensable. When we shall have done a task well, we should tell ourselves that it is the Lord who wished to do us the honor of serving Himself in us, but that in reality, of ourselves we have no right to anything.

. . . *Service with nothing withheld, service without regret:* "No one, having put his hand to the plow and looking back, is fit for the kingdom of God" (Luke 9:62).

. . . *Exclusive service:* With God there is no question of a servant playing a double role. "No man can serve two masters . . ." (Matt. 6:24); "The Lord thy God shalt thou worship and him only shalt thou serve" (Matt. 4:10). The apostles understood this perfectly: One must leave all to follow Him.

. . . His service, and the service He expects from us is *not a mercenary service, but a service of love and by love.* This love is proved by sacrifice unto death, even to the death of the Cross.

Christ Himself will reward all those who follow Him.

. . . He desires *a joyous service.* "Serve the Lord in joy," says Psalm 99. St. Paul will say later: "God loves a cheerful giver" (2 Cor. 9:7).

The humiliations of the servant will be a source of glory and a subject of astonishment for the world:

"Behold my servant shall understand: he shall be exalted and extolled, and shall be exceeding high.

"As many have been astonished at thee, so shall his visage be inglorious among men and his form among the sons of men.

"He shall sprinkle many nations: kings shall shut their mouth at him. For they to whom it was not told of him have seen: and they that heard not have beheld" (Isai. 52:13–15).

There is nothing that can so solidly establish in us the fundamental attitude of the religious soul as the contemplation of Jesus kneeling before His disciples to wash their feet.

Let us hear Him say to us: "I have given you an example, that as I have done to you, so you also should do" (John 13:15).

"God does not give us graces or talents or virtues for

ourselves alone. We are members one of another and everything that is given to one member is given for the whole body." [1]

Whatever may be the type of our service, it is always God whom we serve: God in Himself, God in His poor, God in our Sisters, God in the sick, God in the children, God in the old people, God in His priests, God in His holy will, no matter how disconcerting it may be sometimes to our poor human views.

We must live always in a state of service and prepare always to be able to serve better. There arises the question of evaluating ourselves, even on the human plane or from a technical point of view, but we must not forget that our religious service is at the same time of another order: the order of charity which transcends the order of nature, at the same time that it exalts it.

The great service which God asks of a consecrated soul is above all the service of love.

Each of us has a greater reason than that for living outside of herself: to live for God and for His kingdom. God needs our participation in order that His Redemption may be fully realized.

Works of zeal have less need of physical strength than of hearts generous in humility and in self-sacrifice, conditions necessary in order that God may remedy secretly the deep-seated insufficiency of His apostles.

Colloquy

My daughter, I need you. I need your labors, your fatigues, your prayers, your penances, yes, and your joys also.

Live in a state of oblation. I need your entire life.

There is so much to do to apply to each generation the fruits of My life and of My death . . . There is so much to do to conquer the obstacles in the way, without violating free wills . . . There is so much to do to create that attitude in souls which will make them eager to answer "yes" to My appeal . . .

What concerns Me above all is this: to be served, as much as My heart desires, by souls who are consecrated to Me, so that I may purify, strengthen, sanctify all humanity.

The rest will follow: peace in the world, utilization of the advancements of science for legitimate human happiness, the union of minds and of hearts, better conditions for the seeking of truth and of the spiritual expansion of mankind.

Consecrated souls have a great responsibility. I have a right to count on them. Their eternal joy will be dazzling, but they must help Me on earth: by serving, by struggling, by working, by suffering with Me.

If they do not correspond with their vocations, souls whom they should have helped will be the victims of their defection.

Never will you be sufficiently zealous in the service of souls.

If only you could understand the value of souls, the value of a single soul. . . . Each soul has its place in My heart. Each one is loved for something unique that I have given it, and I am not consoled when a soul fails Me as long as there is a hope that it will repent. For Me the ninety-nine faithful sheep do not take the place of the one that has strayed away. Each soul is for Me an incomparable treasure.

My daughter, keep yourself available and docile, ready for My call to action. Consecrated as you are to My Love, you have a part in the Redemption, which is My great work *par excellence*. From all eternity the Father has chosen you for this end.

If only all consecrated souls would surrender themselves to Me unreservedly. . . . If I did not find so often and so much resistance, defection, betrayal . . . If only I might get from souls the service I have a right to expect . . .

It is in the hearts of My chosen ones that the destinies of the world are worked out, rather than around the tables of diplomats and of the major powers.

If you but knew your importance, your influence, your power . . .

It is not necessary to be famous to influence the world. In reality, I have more need of your obscurity than of your notoriety. I have more need of your patience than of your success.

My logic is far different from that followed by men. Divine views are essentially penetrating; those of men on the surface.

I cling to what exists. Man does not look beyond externals, beyond smoke which is quickly dispersed into space and time.

Each consecrated soul has his type of service which, in a certain sense, is personal to him and incommunicable.

Your mission in the complex and invisible domain of

the Mystical Body is your own, and no one can replace you precisely. The good that you should have done and that you have not done will remain undone eternally. I took you seriously, and it is no slight matter that I chose you.

No one has ever served Me as did My Mother. She has always been and she will ever be *par excellence* the "Servant of the Lord." There is not a gesture of hers, not a thought, not an act, which has not had complete efficacy in cooperating in the salvation of the world, because in her there was never any self-seeking: in her everything was complete service.

Let Me make use of you as I intend. Be pliable. I do not suppress initiative, quite the contrary. Let your service be actuated by supernatural motives, and all that you undertake will serve efficaciously.

There is nothing in you which cannot be of service to Me if you will but do it in a true spirit of service. Everything that is penetrated by love is useful.

How many times I wait for you for Myself . . . for others. . . . Whatever is done apart from Me and My love, is a waste.

Have a devotion to the present moment. Only in that way can you serve Me truly. The past is no more; the future is not here yet. The only instant that you possess and on which you can actually count is the actual present moment.

Utilize to the fullest the moment that you have.

The souls of children need Me so much, and I need you so much to give Me to them. Do not refuse Me the transparent envelope of your humanity by which I can go to them.

It does not suffice that you wish to work for Me by living your life tranquilly according to your own ideas.

What I expect of you is that you live My life while working for Me to help souls.

You have nothing to lose by forgetting yourself. The more you work for Me in souls, the more I will reward you on this earth and the more you will find your true place in My Heart in the full expansion of nature and of grace, while awaiting the day when you will understand, in the splendor of glory, the reason of all things.

As I respect your free will, as I serve Myself through you, do you also respect the liberty of souls as you serve Me in them. From the beginning of the world no two souls have ever been exactly alike. Each has its way of coming to Me. Each soul has its own characteristics. Each has its own pace. The servant is careful to follow the pace of his master or mistress.

The more you keep in the background, the more discreet you are, content to make Me known without pretending to convince souls, the more will I attract them and act in them.

The more you put yourself forward and try to impose on others your tastes, your desires, your methods, your ideas, the more you will thwart My work and My grace.

Practice speaking to people as if you were an inferior.

I, your God, put Myself on My knees to wash the feet of My disciples. Do you, then, humble your soul when you counsel or even when you reprove souls. That will be easy if your faith is keen enough to contact Me in each one.

It is unconscious pride which spoils most of the work of My apostles. That makes even the most ardent zeal go astray, sometimes making it operate in a sense quite contrary to that intended.

I have never shown to sinners or to poor sick souls a condescending or a superior manner. In spirit, on My knees, I have listened to them and I have cured them, and yet I am God.

Keep this in mind: what I want most particularly is you, not your works. It is not the work you do that is most important, but what you let Me do through you.

It is easy to work vigorously before the public. It is very difficult to step back and let Me act.

I exact nothing. I wait.

If work overburdens you, it is because you have neglected Me.

The letter killeth; it is I who give life, which dominates matter, work, and time.

Examen

1. Have I understood that the greater my responsibilities the more I must consider my mission of teaching a service?

2. Do I consider my title of teacher a reason for devoting myself humbly, without any self-seeking? (All self-seeking leads to the thwarting of grace of which I should be the channel.)

3. Am I truly convinced that I am not on this earth to be happy, but to be useful, and that I shall find happiness the more if I do not try to make it for myself, but try to make others happy, at the same time that I help them to become better?

4. Am I really persuaded that there is only one thing which matters: the increase of Christ in the world? Have I understood that, according to the word of Saint John the Baptist, He must increase, I must decrease? The essential thing is that He be loved; the important thing is that good be done; the necessary thing is that "His Kingdom Come" in every house that I direct, in all souls confided to me. *Oportet illum regnare:* "He must reign."

5. Have I understood thoroughly that if I seek myself in the apostolate under any form whatsoever, in the satisfaction of self-love, in an anxious desire for esteem and for affection, in the need of consolation, the hope of gratitude, I shall find myself, perhaps, but in truth, I shall find only nothingness? . . .

On the contrary, if it is God whom I seek, that is to say, if I seek to have His will better understood and fulfilled, His truth better recognized and assimilated, His life more appreciated and imitated, it is God whom I find; and in Him I find the secret of expansion, of real joy, since He is then my true reason for working and for suffering. For an educator, esteem and consolation, under whatever guise they present themselves, can be sometimes the consequence or the providential recompense of her action, never an end. The only end: Christ in souls.

6. Have I not had the experience that disinterested service to souls is the condition even of securing their confidence, and that, very often, the fact of considering authority as a service takes away from the tone of the voice and from the general attitude all that rudeness, severity, and, let us say the word: a tendency to authoritarianism, which a commanding manner can betray?

7. Does not the idea that we are only servants, and even useless servants whom the Lord might disregard, make humility easier, and likewise detachment, when providential circumstances oblige us to retire?

8. Is it not this attitude which draws down many blessings on our work, since God is pleased to intervene when His instruments do not seek to attribute to themselves the glory of the good He permits them to do?

Resolutions

1. To consider the authority which is granted to me by the office which I hold as a service, and not as an essential faculty.

2. To accept the honors due to my rank or to my charge as being addressed, not to me personally, but to the authority of God, whom I represent.

3. To kneel often before the souls whom I have been commissioned to serve and to educate.

4. By the very fact of my vocation as an educator, I do

not belong to myself; I ought, therefore, to be ready to go always where God calls me without reflecting on my desires or on my whims.

5. To avoid speaking of myself and of what I do, even to speak ill of myself. The "I" of an educator is the most odious of all. The more the "I" disappears, the more Christ will be apparent.

6. To be on one's guard against the use of the possessive: "My" work, "my" pupils; to use it only with a corrective, at least interiorly. I forget so easily that the children belong to God, to their parents, and . . . to themselves.

7. In dealing with souls to develop the approach which includes ardent zeal for souls, and at the same time a respect for their freedom.

8. At this epoch of the world when buying and selling are so stressed, to teach the children to appreciate the beauty of little services rendered gratuitously, "through love," without hope of reward.

9. Whenever an occasion presents itself, to extol the royalty of the spirit of service.

PRAYER

Lord Jesus, who came to earth not to be served but to serve, teach me to serve You in souls as You want me to do. Preserve me from all self-seeking. Keep my heart detached from all spiritual pride. Grant me grace never to attribute to myself the good that You allow me to do. Grant that I may be so filled with Your spirit and Your Love, that in giving myself, I may really give You.

AMEN

CHAPTER V

Daughters of the Church

They say that on her deathbed, in an overflowing joy of ecstasy, St. Teresa of Avila repeated frequently and with clearness and majesty: "Lord, I am a daughter of the Church."

Was this a final protest against the false accusations of denunciators who had so often pursued her to the tribunal of the Inquisition?

Was it the memory of all she had accomplished by the Reform of Carmel, for the defense of the Church against the Lutherans, and for the expansion of the Church in missionary countries? (Is it not said that by her penance she converted more pagans than did St. Francis Xavier?)

Would it not rather be because in her humility, in the light of eternity, she was proclaiming the truth of that axiom which is so falsely interpreted: "Outside the Church there is no salvation"? All that she had received, all that had sanctified her, all that had helped her to answer the divine call, *all* had been received through the Church.

In her humility, considering herself a small part of the great ensemble so rich in her eyes, she slips into her place at the solemn hour of truth, the hour of death, and proclaims joyfully, proudly, gratefully: "Lord, I am a daughter of the Church." [1]

A precious lesson for all religious souls. Beyond all the distinctions of orders or of nations, St. John Chrysostom says that it is our pride, our hope, our salvation to belong to the Church of Jesus Christ, which outstrips space and time, which unites us within to all our human family and yet more to the most human of all our brothers, God Himself, the Word Incarnate.

Thérèse of Lisieux understood this very well, she who was so remarkable for her pilgrimage to Rome. She used to say: "I am a Child of the Holy Church. My glory is in the light that radiates from the forehead of my Mother."

At this time when the Church is the object of so many persecutions, oppositions, misunderstandings, is it not fitting that we be more conscious of our membership in the Church, and that in all love we become truly a fundamental part of her?

The whole object of this meditation is to help us to develop in the young people on whom we have influence a deep pride in the fact that they are daughters of the Church, that they owe an obedience and a respect to its leaders, the visible representatives of Jesus Christ on earth.

Meditation

Let us adore our Lord founding the Church and assembling the first apostolic group after having spent the night in prayer on the mountain.

Let us listen as He likens His Church to a sheepfold: "And other sheep I have that are not of this fold. Them also I must bring, and they shall hear my voice, and there shall be one fold and one shepherd" (John 10:16).

Let us listen to Him as He promises unfailing assistance: "Thou art Peter, and upon this rock I will build my Church, and the gates of hell shall not prevail against it" (Matt. 16:18); "I am with you all days, even unto the consummation of the world" (Matt. 28:20); "Whatever thou shalt bind on earth shall be bound in heaven" (Matt. 16:19); "He who hears you, hears me; and he who rejects you, rejects me" (Luke 10:16).

Let us reflect on some of the following thoughts:

God, who is the source of love, has created us in love to share in the Church, in His life of love and of unity.

This communal assumption, whereby God shares His love in common with all members of the Church, does not prevent complete intimacy with God (fraternal love does not prevent filial love). But our vocation is not only a personal sharing in the communal divine love, but a sharing with all others.

Eternal happiness will result from this double love: love of God and mutual love. The two are essential and strengthen each other. Our joy will be the greater that we shall be loving God together, and that we shall love one another with the same love with which He loves each of us. This fraternal love will be the more ardent in that on earth we worked *together* to establish a communion of love to prepare that eternal Church.

The circle of love which constitutes the Trinity is opened wide in Christ to unite humanity. The history of the world is the necessary duration for this embrace. When Christ will come again, the circle will be closed definitely on the elect of humanity sharing as a family in the Church, in the life, in the glory, in the joy of God.

In other words, the Church is composed of the people of God on the way to be taken up by Christ Jesus to be put by Him into the Family of the Blessed Trinity.

"It is my belief that Jesus Christ and the Church are one," said Joan of Arc with her intelligent and lively faith. There is no such thing as Jesus Christ on one side, the Church on the other. The Church is not a body foreign to Christ; it is His Body in a state of growth, nourished, vivified by Him, according as each one acknowledges its existence.

Individualism is in formal opposition to the Christian spirit. The same grace incorporates us in Christ and in the Church. The same vital current which binds us to the Church binds us to all the other members of Christ. It is from the Body of Christ that we receive life. It is for this Body that we must work and live, since we are one of its elements. "For the body is not one member, but many.

If the foot says, 'Because I am not a hand, I am not of the body,' is it therefore not of the body? And if the ear says, 'Because I am not an eye, I am not of the body,' is it therefore not of the body?" (1 Cor. 12:15-17).

In short, it is the same Jesus who is all in all, pope in the sovereign pontiff, bishop in his excellency, pastor in M. le curé, superior in reverend mother, sister cook in our little sister in the kitchen, penitent in each repentant sinner, preacher in each missionary, conqueror of Satan in that youth struggling with temptations, sufferer in that sick person, the humiliated one in that cripple, etc. And each, while receiving according to his deeds, that is, according to his fidelity to grace, will share in the glory and happiness of the others. Ste Thérèse of the Infant Jesus spoke of the joy which those souls will experience whose life on earth has been apparently obscure and useless, when they will understand, in the day of revelation, that a certain act of love they made once will have contributed to the holiness of a great saint. Every one who belongs to the great ensemble of the Church must contribute to the happiness of the whole body.

The Church is a mother. The Church produces divine life, but not in the same way as humanity, in which birth consists, for the child, in leaving the womb of its mother. On the contrary, baptism is an incorporation in the Church, an entrance into the Church, an insertion into the Church. You know the classic passage from Bossuet: "Happy Motherhood of the Church! Mothers whom we see on earth in truth conceive their fruit in their womb, but they give birth by removing the child from the womb. On the contrary, Holy Church conceives outside and gives birth inside her womb." She must give, then, her universal presence to every man coming into this world in order to give him divine life. She must give birth in divine life to all humanity, and guard each soul in her womb to unite it to Christ. That is the whole problem of the apostolate. Beyond even visible borders, the Church exercises her maternal mission. Grace, which animates every man of good will, comes from Christ through the maternal heart of the Church.

Seen from outside, the Church may seem to some people an enigma, a disorder, a scandal. The contemporaries of Christ were scandalized by hearing God spoken of as a man who ate and drank with others. (Let us remember that it was forbidden to them to make images of God and even to pronounce His name, and yet here was a being of flesh and blood called God.) We must look at the Church from within, with the eyes of faith. Paradoxes and oppositions are reconcilable in a superior plan.

Seen from outside, a stained glass window seems incoherent, precisely because it has not been designed to be viewed from without but from within. To understand the window one must enter the edifice. Then there is no longer a problem; all is clear. The dark spots of the window now seem an integral part of its beauty.

We must cling to Christ just as we find Him. We must accept Him completely, otherwise we do not accept Him at all. One cannot divide Christ and choose Him in part. Faith in the Church is part of our faith in Christ.

The Church holds promises of eternity and the assurance of assistance from the Holy Spirit. Divine in her Founder, in her sacraments, in her doctrine, she is yet human in her rulers and in her members. She has submitted to the earthly law of struggle, of effort, of progress. There is in her enough light and sanctity so that compliance to the Church even from a human point of view is possible, if there are enough deficiencies and shadows so that there may be merit in our loyalty to her. According as one is united to the Church as the branch is united to the trunk, one receives the maximum amount of the sap which rises from the roots and which produces fruits. Those who have separated from the Church under a pretext that she does not measure up to their personal ideas, have ended in emaciation and ruin.

We must use the first person when we speak of the Church. We are in the Church as we are in Christ. We must find joy and pride in belonging to the Church, but always with humility. No one is exclusive in his membership. Our belonging to the Church entails a responsibility to strive for greater love and holiness.

Colloquy

My daughter, because you are My daughter, by that very fact you are a daughter of My church, for the Church and I are one.

Think of yourself as a living cell in the Body which is My Church. You are a part of this great ensemble to which you owe everything and for which you owe everything.

By your religious profession, in response to My appeal, you have freely and totally consecrated yourself to the service of the Church. In fulness and with a clear conscience, you have ratified the donation of your baptism. Take this consecration seriously. You do not belong to yourself any longer; you belong to the Church.

Act, pray, work, not for your own advancement, nor even for the sole profit of your religious congregation, but for the benefit of the whole Church through your congregation. Forget yourself. Work with Me for the great interests of Christianity. Have a special care, first of all, for My growth in all souls, then particularly in those souls who apparently are separated from Me.

Working, praying, suffering, if you are united to the Church, your power is great, for your activity, as well as your prayer and suffering, become Mine.

While enlarging your heart to embrace the whole world, while sharing all with the universal Church, you will overcome more easily the meannesses of daily life, you will understand how truly particularism and sectarianism are harmful and ridiculous things; you will breathe the air freely; you will feel the great breath of My Spirit pass through your soul.

There is a great grace for which I am asked all too seldom, one which is of capital importance: it is the grace of union of heart with superiors. It is through her superiors that a religious is attached to the Church. There is nothing that the devil fears so much. That is why he multiplies causes of misunderstandings and of variance. The more, however, that a religious is united to her congregation and the more the congregation itself is united to the hierarchy, the more the sap passes from the trunk into the branches to bear abundant fruit for the glory of My Father.

Whoever is truly united to the Church works efficaciously in the field of souls, even if the success is not apparent. He who acts according to his own judgment, without thought of his communion with the Church, can give himself much trouble and cause some disturbance, but he wears himself out without benefitting anyone, unless it be the devil . . .

This is hard to understand, I know: one is so apt to circumscribe his horizons, to fold himself up in his own work. But truth frees one. Daughter of the Church, it is with the whole Church that you must struggle and rejoice.

You must espouse deliberately the great intentions of My Church: missionary acuteness; the return to the fold of so many lost sheep; the return to unity under the crook of the Supreme Shepherd of so many separated brethren; the re-Christianization of the realm of the working man; the end of persecutions; peace among nations in justice and in love; but above all, the sanctity of My apostles. That is one of the specific functions of the religious. In the retreat preparatory to the first Pentecost, I desired that My disciples be helped by the praying presence of My Mother and of the holy women. The holiness of My priests continues to depend in large part on the fervor with which consecrated souls continue the feminine mission begun in the Cenacle, a truly spiritual maternity which prolongs the sacerdotal maternity of Mary.

Examen

1. Do I live with the Church, making her interests my interests, showing concern for her growth, for her purity, for her sanctity?

2. Do I pray with the Church, loving and studying her liturgy, uniting myself with all those who pray in the name of those who do not pray?

3. Do I offer with the Church the incessant oblation of Jesus, prolonged as it is by the sacrifices of all the members of the Mystical Body?

4. Do I suffer with the Church, suffering in my heart her wounds, sharing also by my labors in that mysterious maternity which never ceases to bring forth many children into the life of grace, or which revives those who have lost that life?

5. Do I humble myself with the Church, doing penance with her for those who are corrupted and who so shamelessly sully others?

6. Do I believe with the Church, knowing that while she is human in her members, she is divine in her Founder, in her doctrine, in her mission?

7. Do I understand that it is normal to have in the Church defects which are the work of men who are members of the Church? Far from being scandalized, do I see in that the refinement of the Saviour who wished to make the faithful and the pastors realize that they must give an example of effort, that they should experience struggle, that they should be stirred up to special prudence and self-control, that they should never feel satisfied nor relax in a false tranquillity?

8. Do I work with the Church in the way desired by the hierarchy, ardently hopeful to enter lovingly into

their views and humbly intelligent in following their directives?

9. Do I rejoice with the Church? Am I happy in her progress, joyful in her feasts, proud of her accomplishments, of her victories?

10. Do I hope with the Church, knowing that in her militant phase she must struggle against the forces of evil, with alternating advances and failures, but confident that the infernal powers can never prevail against her? Nothing that will have been done with her, in her, and for her will have been lost.

11. Do I make every effort to develop in my pupils an enlightened understanding and a fervent love of the Church, and a pride without arrogance in the fact that they belong to the Church, and a desire to know her better and to serve her more perfectly?

Resolutions

1. To belong sincerely to the Body of the Church. As daughter of the Church, I become one with her. It is by her that I become one with Christ.

2. To feel more and more my incorporation with the Church. Whatever concerns her, concerns me; whatever harms her, harms me.

3. To take to heart that I am not an isolated individual, but a member of a great ensemble. To unite myself with the entire Church to pray, to offer, to work.

4. To accept loyally my responsibility as a daughter of the Church. Without being the whole Church, a religious teacher represents a part of the Church in her special sphere of action. Her conduct can make the affection of young people for the Church either increase or decrease.

5. To show a deferential submission to the directives of the Church in every circumstance, in little things as in great.

6. Never to criticize nor, as far as my authority extends, permit others to criticize the rulers of the Church: beyond their person, there is their office; beyond their office, there is Christ Himself.

7. To try to give to young people a complete, enthusiastic knowledge of the Church. To stir up their interest in the great religious problems. To inculcate in them a spirituality that is essentially ecclesiastical, totally penetrated with a communal and a missionary charity, a charity without any partisan spirit.

8. To make them realize that the parish is the spiritual and temporal place of their environment in the Church. To inspire them with obedience and gratitude toward the clergy, with an interest in the development of priestly vocations, with a desire to participate progressively in the liturgical life of the Church and in its apostolic activities, as well in the plan of Catholic Action as in the program of charity.

PRAYER

Holy Virgin Mary, you who watched over the first steps of the infant Church, instill into our hearts an immense love for holy Church. You who suffered so much in your heart during the first persecutions against the Church, give courage and strength to those who today struggle and suffer for her. You whose prayer is so powerful over the heart of your Son, obtain for all our brothers and sisters who have strayed from the Church the grace to return to the unity of the apostolic and Roman faith. You who prayed so much with the holy women for the apostles, sanctify all our priests and develop in us the spirit of respect and of obedience toward them. Make us completely zealous under the direction of our superiors in the service of the Church, which prolongs here below your well-beloved Son, who lives and reigns with the Father in the unity of the Holy Spirit, forever and ever.

AMEN

CHAPTER VI

The Missionary Spirit

A religious without a missionary spirit is a religious without an understanding of the religious life.

Though it be a contemplative life in which no external apostolic activity is possible, her religious life has significance only if, having really grasped the immense majesty of God, she desires to work from within for the sanctification of His name and the coming of His kingdom throughout the whole earth.

But if she is a religious teacher, she has the further responsibility of the Christian formation of a certain number of young souls. She must not forget the words of Pope Pius XI: "There is authentic and complete Christian education only where there is an understanding of the missionary life so profound that it penetrates the life of the youth when he attains maturity."

Too often this missionary education, without a solid foundation and sure techniques, amounts to little more than some pretty costume parties, to little more than stirring stories of savages, more or less romanticized; in fine, it amounts to little more than a child's pretty plays, which at most stir up the imagination.

As a teacher imparts ideals only insofar as she lives them, a meditation on this subject may help us to awaken a true missionary consciousness, and at the same time it may help us to meet more efficiently the requirements of our vocation.

Meditation

Let us adore our Lord, who desires to make us share in His immense zeal to glorify His Father and to share His divine life with all humanity.

"I do not seek my own glory; there is one who seeks and who judges" (John 8:50).

"I came that they may have life, and have it more abundantly" (John 10:10).

Let us note in passing how these two points are related. The glory of God does not consist essentially in an exterior manifestation, in a sort of military parade or a superficial triumph, but in that interior vivifying of men, freely accepted by them, which enables the Incarnate Word to give Himself to them by love and at the same time to unite them to Him in the constant oblation He makes of Himself in homage to His Father.

"A living man is the glory of God," St. Irenaeus used to say. God uses His glory to vivify man, and man finds the joy of his life in glorifying God.

In that spirit let us review all the Gospel texts referring to missionaries: the Parable of the Good Shepherd; the entire tenth chapter of St. John; "I have compassion on the crowd . . ." (Mark 8:2).

"I have come to cast fire upon the earth . . ." (Luke 12:49); "The Son of Man has not come to be served but to serve and to give his life as a ransom for many" (Matt. 20:28); "I have chosen you, and have appointed you that you should go and bear fruit . . ." (John 15:16); "Go into the whole world and preach the gospel to every creature . . ." (Mark 16:15).

Let us recall from the Gospel some noted texts of St. Paul: "Woe to me if I do not preach the gospel!" (1 Cor. 9:16); "God our Savior . . . wishes all men to be saved and to come to the knowledge of the truth" (1 Tim. 2:4); "The love of Christ impels us . . ." (2 Cor. 5: 14).

And now let us reflect on the following thoughts:

Our religious life has for an essential foundation the appreciation of the absolute greatness of God. "How good is God," Ampère used to say to young Ozanam. "God is so great that one greater there cannot be. God is so good that one better there cannot be," St. Louis had already said to de Joinville. Who among us has not meditated on that famous sentence spoken by Jesus to St. Catherine of Siena: "I am He who is; thou art she who is not . . ."

A religious soul is one that has been impressed by the absolute in God to the point where she must detach herself from all else to consecrate herself entirely to Him.

At the same time that she gives herself to God without reserve, however, the religious soul cannot but be shocked by the most alarming scandals and she cannot but recognize the immense "stupidity" of so many men, in whom God, the essential Being, has so little place, while their thoughts are dominated by those vain and empty things they call honor, wealth, and pleasure.

This wounding of the soul of the religious is changed

into an impulse of double pity: pity for Him who is Love itself and who is so little loved; pity for our human brothers who live on earth so that they scarce know what they do. It is this double impulse of double pity which engenders the missionary sense. A call to life in a mission field is a particular vocation, but missionary consciousness is an integral part of every religious vocation.

Missionary awareness is nothing else than deep concern for everything which concerns the progress of the Church in the world, joined to the desire to contribute to it according to one's means.

This is merely a normal instinct, a logical reflex for every baptized soul which recognizes the fact that she is a child of God and a member of the Mystical Body.

There is no Christian spirit without the missionary spirit. But, reciprocally, one of the surest ways of increasing the Christian spirit in a soul is to develop in it an awareness of the missions.

An education for the missions gives one a feeling for others, makes one grow in charity, makes one appreciate the privilege of being a child of Holy Church.

The feeling for others: We are wont to identify Christianity with the Western elements in the midst of which we have been reared. But, as Pope Pius XII recalls in his encyclical *Evangelii praecones:* "There are other cultures, involving real human values, which must likewise be sanctified, purified, consecrated, that they may be offered to Jesus Christ."

Charity: Egocentricity is our basic tendency. We are inclined to focus our interest on the things which concern us or which are nearest to us, attaching only a relative importance to things which are in another sphere or of another race. The missionary spirit makes us focus on our unity, on our interdependence, on our deep solidarity. Not only does it make us think *of* others, but it makes us think *with* others, so that we may understand them better, respect them more, and love them more sincerely.

The awareness of our membership in the Church: We are privileged beings, and yet we do not give an account of our special favors.

By what right were we born in a Christian family? It might have happened just as well that we would have been born of pagan parents. Every man receives graces sufficient for salvation, but he who is unfaithful to grace has not the same help toward salvation as he who lives in a Christian atmosphere.

Canon Glorieux wrote:

The infidel does not know the infinite goodness of God, His paternity, His fidelity, His promise to hear our sincere prayers.

The infidel does not know Christ, His Incarnation, His Blessed Mother, His patient life, His teaching, His death, His Eucharist, His sacraments, His divine intercession.

The infidel does not know the Church, her history, her saints, her ruler, her creed, her charity.

For the infidel the problem of life, of suffering, of death, remains insoluble.

And he is quite alone with his soul defaced by original sin, alone to meet all the deviations, through perversity or through ignorance, of natural morality; to meet all the weariness, the excuses, the illusions of a conscience abandoned to itself.

But what am I saying? He is not alone, for he is born

and he dies in the midst of a kindred group whose prejudices, whose defects, whose thoughtlessness increase in every generation.

His misery is great, and his salvation uncertain.

Truly he sits in darkness and in the shadow of death.

Our privilege should stimulate us at least to more zeal, for the more we have received, the more will be demanded of us.

"To contribute to the work of the missions . . . that is to give to God a most agreeable proof of one's gratitude for the gift of faith." [1]

"We must recognize the precise obligation of all Christians to cooperate in the work of the missions from the fact that they possess the precious gift of faith, which large masses of the human race do not possess." [2]

"To pay our debts to such a work of charity, according to our means, is to prove that one has a just appreciation of the gift of faith; to pass on this gift, the most precious of all gifts, and all the benefits which go with it, to unfortunate pagans, is to proclaim our gratitude to the Divine Goodness . . ." [3]

After nineteen centuries of Redemption, at this moment there are still more than one thousand millions of pagans.

Is that the fault of Jesus Christ? Certainly not. What more could He have done?

Must it not be, then, the fault of Christians who have not understood their responsibilities?

"All the faithful for all the infidels," such was the watchword of Pope Pius XI, who added: "Help to the missions is a duty which obligates according to the possibilities of each individual."

Undoubtedly infidels of good faith and of good will benefit by the vital exchanges of the Body of Christ. Unconsciously, invisibly, they belong to the Church. When one thinks, however, of the support that visible membership in the Church brings, and again, of the poverty of so many men who have never heard tell of her—other than in a ridiculous way—how much one wishes that there were enough Catholic missionaries so that all souls of good will might know authentically the Church of Jesus Christ and hear His Message of love and of life.

At the moment there is much talk about peace. With just reason we believe that if a new war comes upon us, it will be even more frightful than the last one. Is one not correct in thinking that if, conforming to the instructions of the sovereign pontiffs, the activity of Christians had been more deliberately oriented toward the missions, charity would have merited for the world escape from the horrible scourge of war? How many efforts and thousands of millions spent in utter loss would have facilitated the expansion of the missions and would have gathered masses of people in the unity of Christ!

As members of the Church we must be zealous for its growth. Do we not pray every day for "the salvation of the whole world"?

We must not establish an airtight wall between the local apostolate and the missionary idea. There is only one great purpose: to help Jesus save the world through the Church.

"Since we are members of a Church which has not

finished its growth, we must all share in helping in its expansion." [4]

To pretend to be a part of Catholic Action and to be concerned only about our immediate surroundings without a strong concern about the complete life of the whole Church, would be as absurd as for a doctor to be interested in one organ and to neglect the rest of the body.

Let us never forget that true missionary work is accomplished as much by interior struggles of holiness as by exterior action. Missionary life is not only a work of instructing; it is even more a struggle between the forces of Christ and the powers of evil. Within each soul is worked out the issue of the spiritual conflict for the liberation of the world.

Colloquy

My daughter, stop all your reflections and reasonings, excellent though they may be.

Come close to Me with a childlike soul, adoring, listening, ready to learn from Me.

When a soul comes thus to me to collect My intimate thoughts, it is not time lost.

Without exception I love all souls very much. They can be counted by the thousands of millions; yet I look upon each one as if there were no one else in the world. I am interested in each one. I study their interior reactions. Discreetly, without infringing on their liberty, I attract each one, I help him, I strengthen him.

What joy fills My heart when they make a choice in

favor of My love! What suffering is mine when the choice is a refusal of all that I want to give to them!

Do you understand the terrible seriousness of human destiny?

It is a serious thing that I have created you with a free will. It is a serious thing that I have united so many souls in this world and made them interdependent.

The exercise of your mutual charity will provide the means for relieving the poverty of your spiritually needy brothers and, at the same time, it will contribute to your advance in the ways of love.

It is only on this earth that you can collaborate meritoriously in the Redemption, and that you can make fruitful My prayer, My suffering, My life, even though your contribution be very modest. Later, it will be eternally too late.

You cannot know how much I thirst for souls, how much—blissful and united in the Holy Trinity—We desire that all be united in Our supreme joy.

Centuries may pass . . . I do not use extreme efforts to draw all souls to Me; I died for them, died after having been scourged, tortured . . . all of which I accepted willingly, when I needed only to make a movement to annihilate My executioners. But I wished to give you the greatest proof of love: to lay down one's life for those one loves.

Help Me. . . . If you do not help Me there is such or such a soul in distress to whom I shall not be able to apply the fruits of the Redemption.

Work at the salvation of souls as if you were saving Me.

Use the opportunities which I put at your disposal, and those which I leave to your initiative.

Ask of Me missionary zeal, which is nothing else than a sharing in the *Sitio* (I thirst) of Calvary.

You are more powerful than you think. So many beneficent and invisible waves emanate from a religious soul which shares the cares of My heart, and which works for the great interests of My Church.

You can help Me by your prayer. Tell Me the names of the souls whom you wish to lead to Me, and tell Me the names of those who are unmindful of Me.

You can help Me by your charity. How can you love the soul of a pagan who needs your sacrifices, if you do not love completely your Sister who is near you and in whom I dwell?

You can help Me by your obedience. It was by being obedient even unto the death of the Cross that I repaired all human disobediences—echoes of the *Non serviam* (I will not serve) of Satan.

Did you enter the religious life that I might realize your desires, or to accomplish Mine?

Help Me by your humility. A soul which humbles itself, even though it be a sinner, is a soul saved.

To obtain for many souls the disposition to humble themselves I permit opportunities to come into your life so that you may humble yourself. Far from discouraging you, they should be for you a reason for thanksgiving.

That is money whose value in precious metal is very high.

If death is the renunciation of life, humiliation is the renunciation of what is most profound in life.

There is only one thing that counts, you see: the victory of Love in each soul. Love—that is My Life. Love—that is My very Self.

Here is one story which is fraught with consequences: the story of the struggle between love and egotism in the kingdom of souls.

Love will prove the stronger. Have confidence, I have overcome the world. In order that love may be strongest in every cell in My Body, however, there must be some chosen souls who will correspond fully in all that I expect from them, and who will transmit to others, in generous portions, My divine radiations.

There are so many souls whom I have chosen for missionary work and who have not responded to My appeal . . . There are so many to whom I have given much, on whom I had a right to rely, but they have let themselves be won over by trifles.

They have not understood the obligations of My gifts. I left them free, even as I respected the liberty of the rich young man.

But what sadness comes from the "No" spoken in opposition to the delicate invitation which I give to My chosen souls.

A little weakness, a fault, a momentary forgetfulness, are small things which do not endanger the work of love, provided that one repairs them by a fresh start as soon as perceived.

What does retard the spread of My kingdom is pride or cowardice, disobedience to lawful superiors, lack of attention to what I ask or to what I inspire, the chronic habit of living in and for exterior things.

What helps Me to conquer the forces of evil, to free captive pagan souls from evil influences, is the "Yes" of a soul who prolongs the *Ecce ancilla Domini* (Behold the handmaid of the Lord), and the *Fiat mihi secundum verbum tuum* (Be it done to me according to Thy word) of My Mother; it is fidelity and—as far as human nature allows—the forgetfulness of self for the good of others; it is the profound union with all the anxieties of My heart.

My daughter, you can be a great missionary soul even if your life is rooted in a restricted task in a limited place.

It is sufficient if your intentions embrace the whole world.

Make an offering to Me of all the men in the whole world. Desire Me. Call upon Me. Aspire after Me in each of them and you will see Me grow in their hearts.

Examen

1. Do I truly thirst for souls?

2. Have I in me something of the desire of St. Paul to make myself all to all to gain all for Jesus Christ?

3. For some time has not my zeal become somewhat chilled, making me do my work in the classroom through duty, in a forced manner, keeping myself tranquil, and making me carry on my apostolate in a routine manner?

4. Is the mainspring of my actions truly a disinterested anxiety to spiritualize the world? Is it not rather like the human desire to exert influence, and the solicitude for my popularity which little by little would

become the real reason for my zeal? Do I understand thoroughly that what counts in the eyes of God is not what appears on the surface? Do I realize that the true good that one does is not always what is apparent?

5. Do I busy myself so much about souls in a sincere desire for their happiness and the delight of God who wishes so much to claim them and to vivify them?

6. Under the pretext that I consecrate to my pupils most of my time, my heart, and my labor, am I not inclined to believe that I have rights over them, and to treat them as a conquered country, forgetting that they do not belong to me?

7. Do I respect sufficiently their liberty and their spontaneity, remembering that God wants before all else from every human creature a spontaneous love?

8. When I have not succeeded as I had hoped, do I not experience spite, discouragement, an inclination to be harsh to unruly children? Am I not tempted to call down fire from heaven, as did the Boanerges (Sons of Thunder), forgetting of what spirit I am?

9. Under the sway of deceptions, of contradictions, of misunderstandings on the part of those who should have done more to help and to encourage me, have I not lost something of my early apostolic fervor, forgetting that the good God does not wish good to be done easily, and that, being called to share in the work of the Redemption, it is quite normal that I find the Cross even in the exercise of charity?

10. Have I special care for the lost sheep, for the distant sheep? Am I not inclined to hedge myself in with a little group of attractive children who give me much consolation? Have I a true, heartfelt interest in souls, in all souls, even in those of whom some say: "They are not interesting"? That is not the mind of Jesus Christ, who for them as for me shed His Blood even to the last drop!

11. Is the thought of souls for me a stimulus to more piety, to more generosity, to more humility? Praying in the name of those who do not pray, humbling myself in the name of the proud, being obedient in the name of those who rebel, doing penance in reparation for the sensual, I nourish with the same virtues of Christ those souls who are my children.

12. Do I realize that the best way to develop the Christian spirit in young people is to make them grow in the missionary spirit? Have I spoken to them of the pontifical missionary projects which are prominent in this era, the Holy Childhood, the Propagation of the Faith? Have I made the problems of the missionary life real to them? Have I stirred up their interest in the cause of God, with love of Him as the motive, remembering the while the respect I owe to the liberty of their consciences?

Resolutions

1. To be definitely aware of great pity for souls and to share with Jesus His thirst for souls.

2. For the love of Jesus to communicate for all souls without exception, to love them as He loves them.

3. To develop a keen sense of my responsibilities: There are hundreds, perhaps thousands, of souls which are connected in some way with mine. I have received for them all that I have received.

4. Frequently to purify my intention for the apostolate: Christ in souls is my reason for all that I do.

5. To offer souls more frequently in the presence of the Blessed Sacrament: "Power went forth from him and healed all" (Luke 6:19).

6. To unite myself frequently with the actual prayer of Jesus for souls in the whole world.

7. To create an atmosphere favorable to the missions, whether at catechism class or in secular studies. To use for this purpose biographies, atlases, missionary games. To have a world map, and to interest my pupils in the progress of the Church.

8. To give them a very authentic idea of the value of a soul. To insist in the recitation of the *Pater* on the missionary sense of the *adveniat regnum tuum* (Thy Kingdom come). To remind them how much more privileged they are than so many pagan children of their age, and to show them the responsibilities which are consequently theirs. To develop in them a pride in a Church like theirs.

9. To tell them of beautiful lives of missionaries, not so much for their picturesqueness, as for the information which shows them as apostles who establish Christi-

anity, and who make known the true Church to those of our far away brothers who have never known of Christianity.

10. To profit by the death of a religious or of a missionary to give them a talk on the missions. Children are always more susceptible to the vital testimony of an eyewitness.

11. To put them in touch with a missionary to whom they will write every month, or with children in a home for orphans.

12. To have them make collections of photographs or of prints depicting the missions, including foreign stamps, all of which can be used for missionary exhibits.

13. To mention the missions often as an intention for prayer and sacrifices: thanksgiving, the rosary, a visit to the Blessed Sacrament, etc. To insist at Mass on the *totius mundi salute,* and the *toto orbe terrarum* (For the salvation of the whole world).

PRAYER

Lord Jesus, who in Your great goodness have chosen me among thousands of others to help You to give Yourself to souls, grant me grace never to disappoint You. Since You wish to depend on me for Your growth in many souls allied to mine, make me understand better Your *Sitio* (I thirst) of Calvary. Enkindle in my heart the fire of Your love; give me an ardent and disinterested missionary zeal, so that without any self-seeking, my life may be consumed in making You known and loved.

AMEN

CHAPTER VII

The Spirit of Peace

If there is a deep longing for anything in the human heart today, it is for peace. Never has peace been talked about so much. Never has there been so much dispute about it. Never have there been so many conventions and conferences about it. And, paradoxically, never has there been so much "fighting" for peace.

If any souls ought not only to desire peace but contribute to establish it, they are consecrated souls. Are they not the spouses of the "Prince of Peace"? Should not they, who have deliberately steered their life toward God, be the living witnesses of divine peace and should they not make their convents and monasteries, according to the saying of St. Benedict, "oases of peace"? Should not they who have for a special mission the making of reparation for the sins of the world, should not they mitigate one of the most certain causes of war on the social plane as on the international plane?

If religious are bound to inculcate the spirit of peace in young people, surely the teaching religious are particularly bound to do this. In fact, while training the hearts and minds of the children, are they not in a certain sense training the hearts and minds of the humanity of tomorrow?

Much prayer and thought should be given to this point, as to that of peace, in line with our providential vocation.

Meditation

Let us adore our Lord greeting us as He loved to greet His disciples: *Pax vobis:* "Peace to you! It is I, do not be afraid" (Luke 24:37).

Let us listen as He tells us just as He told St. John: "Peace I leave with you, my peace I give to you; not as the world gives do I give to you. Do not let your heart be troubled, or be afraid" (14:27); "These things I have spoken to you that in me you may have peace" (16:33). And in St. Mark: "Have salt in yourselves, and be at peace with one another" (9:49).

Let us heed His promise: "Blessed are the peacemakers, for they shall be called the children of God" (Matt. 5:9).

Let us recall the many appeals in St. Paul: "Be of the same mind, be at peace; and the God of peace and love will be with you" (2 Cor. 13:11); "Strive for peace with all men . . . lest any root of bitterness springing up cause trouble and by it the many be defiled" (Heb. 12:14–15); "To no man render evil for evil. . . . If it be possible, as far as in you lies, be at peace with all men" (Rom. 12:17–18); "Bear with one another in love, being careful to preserve the unity of the Spirit in the bond of peace" (Eph. 4:2–3); "May the peace of God which surpasses all understanding guard your hearts and your minds in Christ Jesus" (Phil. 4:7); "May the peace of Christ reign in your hearts; unto that peace, indeed, you were called in one body" (Col. 3:15); "May the Lord of peace himself give you everlasting peace in every place" (2 Thess. 3:16).

Let us try, then, to share this divine peace and, under its influence, let us analyze its elements by classifying our reflections under these points:

    I. What the spirit of peace is not.

   II. What the spirit of peace is.

  III. Conditions for developing the spirit of peace.

I. *WHAT THE SPIRIT OF PEACE IS NOT*

The spirit of peace is not the spirit of tranquillity. St. Thomas gives us this definition of peace, which has become a classic: "Peace is the tranquillity of order." But he never pretended that order was the fruit of tranquillity.

As long as we are on this earth, true order, the fruit of justice, will always be threatened. That is a consequence of original sin, of weakness and of human limitations. To be a passive witness to the assaults of injustice is nothing more nor less than being an accomplice.

In his *Mystery of the Charity of Joan of Arc,* Charles Péguy refers to this contrast between the spirit of peace and the spirit of tranquillity. Madame Gervaise does not hesitate to declare: "From the moment that God calls you, you will never find tranquillity again."

There are some people who put their tranquillity above all else. To live a life that is tranquil, without anxieties, is an ideal unworthy of a noble soul. It is, moreover, an illusory ideal, for life has a way of upsetting those who want to avoid struggle and effort. How could a religious be indifferent to the miseries in the world, to the spiritual and moral distresses of souls, to the sufferings of mankind?

The spirit of peace has nothing in common with Quietism, which is the fruit of a false mysticism, which ends abruptly in self-seeking and in a false conscience, forgetful of the commands of God and of the mission that is hers, fearful of the difficulties of action.

The Hindu cult which, at the moment, tends to infest certain currents of spirituality here and there, is no stranger to this false conception of peace.[1] For the Brahmins, existence is an evil; for them action is the great obstacle to happiness and to salvation. Did not Quietism of the seventeenth century tend, under pretext of absorption in God, to the suppression of personal activity and of moral responsibility?

The spirit of peace is not simply the love of external order. To have order in one's plans, in one's business, in the use of one's time, is a praiseworthy characteristic. But we must mistrust a certain mental distortion which would make us judge a group by the order which reigns in it; which would make us judge of the value of a grouping, or even of a ceremony, by their apparent order. There is an order inspired by fear which is perhaps only an hypocritical peace. Let us recall the celebrated utterance of Minister Sebastiani at the moment when the Polish insurrection of 1831 had been suppressed in waves of blood by the Russians: "Order reigns in Warsaw."

This kind of order is nothing more than the assemblage

of the privileges of a caste or of a class. Of what worth is a "moral order" which is paid for by the misery and suffering of a great number of men? It is not a question of the distress of the world weighing on our nerves, but it is a question of being from the depths of our hearts concerned with the renewal of the face of the earth, and of contributing to it by our effective faith, hope, and charity.

It is not "Pilatism." Pontius Pilate is not dead. Pilatism is the temptation of all those who have a little authority: fear of complications, fear of being compromised, fear of becoming involved.

To be sure, it is not a question of becoming involved carelessly. When one has the honor and the responsibility of being a leader, he should know how, without "Don Quixotism," to protect his subordinates, to be a credit to his signature, to regard his word as good as a written document, to defend those who are unjustly accused.

It is easy enough to slide out of any difficulty, to get out of a scrape, but it is cowardly, and there is a cowardliness that kills. Until the end of the world humanity will associate the name of Pontius Pilate with the sufferings and death of Jesus Christ.

It is not pacificism, enduring all and granting all, abdicating *a priori* at the least sign of opposition, going so far as to forget responsibilities connected with an assignment and with a mission.

Cardinal Feltin said: "Peace is not a matter of sentiment. We do not want a sentimental peace. It has been the cause of too many tears and of the shedding of too much blood. It has been tranquillized too much by hypocrisy, furthered too much by illusions. . . . Let us not lead peace in to the bogs of the Utopian pacificists." [2]

We find in Léopold Levaux:

"Peace is a great benefit. Yes, it is a great good, but not the greatest good," said Père Lebbe, who paid for this statement with his life. "There is another good more precious still and more absolutely essential to man: It is justice . . . A peace which is not based on justice is a false peace, a deceitful, short-lived peace. A peace bought at the price of slavery is a disgrace; life purchased at the price of this disgrace is not worth living; it is nothing more than a slow death. This choice for a Christian would be the worst of forfeitures, for it is the ignoble sin of cowardice, of flight before duty to save one's skin." [3]

II. *WHAT THE SPIRIT OF PEACE IS*

It is the spirit of communion with God, which is supreme peace. God is infinite peace because He is infinite love. In effect, peace is the fruit of love. It is in love that the Three Persons are infinitely discernible and intimately united: the Father, who gives Himself to the Son; the Son, who incessantly receives all from the Father and offers Himself in return to the Father; the Spirit, who is the substantial fruit of this mutual gift. Far from being in opposition to one another, the Three Divine Persons, having only one nature, live in the most perfect harmony. God is peace because He is love, and love leads to unity.

It is in compliance with the plan of God for men. Each soul created to the image of God receives with his nature his place in the world and all the graces to carry out the divine plan in his regard, the sources of his individual peace, and by that same place in the midst of other creatures, the source of peace with his surroundings. Men can have peace only if they agree to work together through a filial and a fraternal love, by the plan of God for each and for all. In other words, the more they have at heart the desire to love God and to accomplish His will, the more surely will the opportunities grow for peace in the world.

It is the desire to know more in order to understand more; to understand more in order to love more; to love more in order to help more all of mankind, far and near. Sometimes it is easier to help those far away than those near at hand. . . . But who would be able to get along with the whole world if he cannot be considerate of his nearest neighbors?

Finally, it is the habitual inclination to keep down to moderate proportions the misunderstandings which inevitably occur among men; and it is the determination to settle them in an atmosphere of loyalty, of equity, of understanding, all of which does not exclude firmness when necessary.

III. *CONDITIONS FOR DEVELOPING THE SPIRIT OF PEACE*

Peace on earth is always an uncertain peace. It is the dream of humanity, for man is a finite being, subject to error and sin. The wages of sin are death, sickness, and even war. On all sides, as St. Peter warned us, the enemy prowls around us. The strengthening of our faith will be the best assurance of our resistance. On earth, however, there is never any definite, any perfect peace. There is a very certain peace at our door, nevertheless—the only peace possible, which we must make a part of ourselves by communion in His spirit of peace.

Peace is one of those benefits which depends on an atmosphere which is the result of a communal effort.

It is not a simple problem, but its solution, at least its relative solution, can be advanced by an attitude of soul penetrated with love.

Even if peace cannot be a definite and universal conquest, one can at least share in creating a breathable atmosphere, one easier for mutual esteem. This can be done by developing feelings of brotherhood, by getting rid of reasons for suspicion, by showing in all circumstances a will sincere in justice, in respect, in dignity toward all men, with consideration for the powers, the needs, the merits of each and of all. To have peace, is anything else necessary?

Most certainly we should pray for peace, for peace is a gift of God. As His Eminence Cardinal Feltin said at Assisi in 1952: "If peace has need of God, God has need of men. The world will belong to those who will love Him more."

All Christian virtues contribute more or less to peace in consciences, in homes, in society, in the whole world.

The spirit of justice is a source of peace. First, there is justice toward God. On the first Christmas night the angels sang: "Glory to God in the highest, and on earth peace among men of good will" (Luke 2:14). The two parts of that sentence are related. The more men work for the glory of God, the more they find peace increasing in their hearts. The more they obey the commandments of God, the more they suppress the principal causes of disunion among men.

There is also the question of justice toward one another. A peace based on injustice is a deceitful peace. A peace imposed by constraint is not peace. There only is peace where no legitimate right is violated. Only as the number increases on all levels of those who protect justice can we hope for the progress of peace. The partisan spirit, the sectarian spirit, the spirit of vengeance are opposed to the spirit of peace.

Humility is a source of peace. Père Robert de Langeac wrote:

Genuine peace is impossible without humility. Learn gradually to despise yourself sincerely before God, or at least make the attempt to do so; you will soon see the fruits of this. If you could attain to a deliberate love of humiliation and opposition you would have made a great step forward on the way to God. Accept simply the little humiliations of every day, without questioning, interiorly or exteriorly. Just try it, and you will see that only the first step is really difficult. You may even develop the habit to a perfect degree and this will be a great source of joy and peace. . . . Be humbly content with not pleasing everybody: to will the contrary would be to will the impossible.[4]

Discretion is a source of peace. The religious, guardian of so many secrets, in touch with so many things, must try more than any one else to avoid whatever might cause enmity among people. An imprudent word can set a home on fire; indiscretion can unsettle lives.

"A soul at peace is a soul that does not tell tales, that does not get involved in tales, that does not listen to tales," Mother Marie Thérèse used to say. She added: "Someone pains me; I will not tell another about it, I will not even tell myself." [5]

Obedience is a source of peace. He who lives in a state of obedience is sure to be in order, since he is assured of doing the will of God. He who resists, suffers and is worn out by his resistance without gain to anyone. His suffering, as it is not the type which atones, which increases love, runs the risk of being a barren suffering.

Moderation is a quality of peace. Much time is spent on efforts which leave the soul bruised and impoverished because they reach out to an ideal in virtue and in sanctity which God does not ask of them. Most certainly, God is mindful of their generosity, but their unwise endeavors do not produce the fruits they hoped for and which would have been theirs if they had been more attentive to what God expected of them, rather than to their own desires.

According to the advice of St. Paul: "Let no one rate himself more than he ought, but let him rate himself according to moderation, and according as God has apportioned to each one the measure of faith" (Rom. 12: 3).

In the French-Latin Breviary published by Labergerie, Père Roguet comments thus on this advice under the date of January eighth: "Not to strive after perfection by means more perfect in themselves than those which are suited to our amount of faith and grace. Works are the nourishment of our soul life. The most perfect works are not in themselves the most perfect for us always. Let us follow humbly but let us not try to outstrip the Holy Spirit."

Contemplation is a source of peace. François René de Chateaubriand wrote:

Prayer is the first of all the duties of man. . . . Neither empires, nor power, nor wars, nor family interests, nor national interests, not one of these weighs one iota in the balance with the great question which is put to each of us: What do you think of prayer? . . . What are you doing in your prayer life? . . .

The more contemplatives there will be, the fewer efforts will be scattered in fruitless strivings. General activity will be the more ordered. From this divine regime society will win as a prize "peace," not the peace of men, which is only animal corpulence, but the peace of God, which surpasses all understanding.[6]

Here it is that enlightened faith which makes us see in every man our brother in Christ, a cell of His Mystical Body, which makes us consider as done to Christ whatever is done to each one. Here it is that enlightened faith facilitates the development of the spirit of peace.

Père Ranwez said:

The Mystical Body is the harmonious ensemble of that human multitude which, united to Christ, reveals Him in a multiple and varied manner. The natural perfection of humanity was a "recapitulation" in each man of every other man, in such a way that each one reveals in his own individual way the rest of humanity. Supernatural perfection is essentially union with Him in whom humanity finds its supreme achievement. It is union with all men. Peace among men, according to Christ, is in the harmony of all men united and sanctified by Christ.[7]

Charity especially is the foundation of every valid effort for true peace. Charity alone enables us to understand the point of view of others, to respect their rights in all justice, and to facilitate harmony while creating an atmosphere of confidence, of understanding, and of union. Charity alone rounds off the angles which an all too brutal justice would make galling. Charity alone helps us to discover points of harmonious approach and to dispel discords.

We shall be workers for peace insofar as we shall be messengers of true charity, of that charity which pardons, which gives, which sacrifices itself.

Colloquy

My daughter, I want you for a few moments of silence and of calmness. I need to speak to you in solitude.

Let all the noises of earth die down gently . . .

It is within that I wish to converse with you. . . . Seek Me in everything and forget all that is not directed to Me . . .

And now listen to Me carefully. Keep your soul in peace, without worry, without fear, without solicitude.

I am the source of peace in you. Drink from that source, taste of that water, let it penetrate to every part of your being: Peace, that is I.

I give you My peace. I leave you My peace. . . . May peace be with you . . .

In saying that I give Myself to you. Breathe Me. . . . Welcome Me. . . . Receive Me. . . . Guard Me and keep Me in your soul.

Then you will know the secret of interior tranquillity. You will receive the grace of profound steadfastness.

Why are you troubled? Are you afraid of Me? Am I not near you, with you, in you?

Your sins, your resistances to grace, your negligences are without number? . . . Yes . . . Humble yourself, accuse yourself honestly, but do not lose your peace, or, if you do lose it, come to Me to recover it in Me. Am I not He who dwells within you, He who, as soon as you regret a fault, excuses it, pardons it, and takes it on Himself? Am I not He who dwells within you, who sees your efforts, your trials, your acts of love; am I not He who weighs them according to their real worth?

I take into consideration your virtues much more than your faults. I look upon your faults only to apply My power to cure you insofar as you desire to be cured. Your virtues are for Me positive approaches of your will in recognition of My gifts which have spread their roots in your soul like pathways of grace. Do not drag your past after you constantly. Confide it once for all to My mercy and cast yourself spontaneously, just as you are, into My arms, that you may enjoy My peace there.

Do not be surprised at your daily miseries. You are not surprised when you have to remove dust every day from a table. . . . Do not be surprised, then, that you must remove dust from your soul every day. I pay more attention to the warmth of your welcome than to the fastidious appearance of your household. Pride and self-seeking can sometimes shine in artificial purity, a purity more apparent than real. Many lose their peace of soul striving after a preparation for Me so perfect that they forget the Host whom they are expecting.

Many, too, lose peace of soul as soon as they no longer feel around them sympathy, confidence, or love.

Be not like them. Most certainly, sympathy, confidence, affection are great benefits. I do not ask you to despise them nor to reject them, but to put your peace above them.

If any one ill-treats you, leave the matter to Me. Let Me have the joy of defending you when I wish, as it pleases Me. If you suffer too much, thank Me for associating you with the work of the Redemption and you will recover peace.

Be not concerned about the future. It is only the present moment that you can sanctify. There is enough pain for each day. For each pain there is enough grace.

Do your daily task well, through love. That will be the best way to prepare for the task of tomorrow.

Be not worried about your relatives. Think more often of My interests and I shall take care of all who are dear to you, better care than you could take of them. Have you not noticed that whatever I protect is well protected?

Bring union and peace wherever you go. Peace should be your gift to every one you meet, to every activity in which you take part.

There is a way of acting and speaking which disturbs and disrupts harmony. There is a way of acting and of speaking which pacifies and creates an atmosphere of serenity.

Ask Me the secret of it. It is a secret of confidence and of love. Such a small thing can change an atmosphere sometimes: a little gentleness and humility, the remembrance of My Presence . . . calm is restored . . .

The spirit of peace is sometimes contagious. It is like a perfumed oil which lubricates and scents from place to place. But it is the heart which distills it and secretes it drop by drop. When all our thoughts, all our feelings, all our desires are saturated with it, then it is diffused, then it spreads to groups and to communities. To transform a whole area only a handful of souls penetrated with it would be needed.

Divine peace is found in the heart of God. As the child develops little by little in the womb of its mother, so do you in the heart of God. Develop in Me, grow in Me, breathe in Me. Be nourished by My thought, by My love, by My holiness, by My desires, so that you may live in Me.

Then you will receive peace unchangeable, the peace which the world cannot give, but which through you and through all souls united to Me I will give to the world.

Examen

1. Am I at peace with God . . . with my conscience . . . with those around me?

2. Do I live in an atmosphere of calmness or of agitation?

3. Do I accomplish everything with diligence but without precipitation?

4. Have I not observed that when I lose peace, I lose my union with God and my authority with my pupils?

5. Am I more impatient than formerly? Have I not noticed that this impatience diminishes my authority

and brings about no good result? Instinctively, children sense very quickly that a person incapable of governing her nerves wastes her rights and her time in directing others.

6. Am I thoroughly persuaded that a teacher should never give the impression of being overwrought, and still less should she speak of it? In the end she would cripple her usefulness.

7. Everyone makes a mistake or commits a fault at times. Those who do nothing are the only ones who never make a mistake.
Have I learned, however, that the surest way to repair error is precisely not to lose my calmness?

8. Am I convinced that there is no fruitful action in feverish agitation? It is better to do a little less but very well, than to do much poorly, for then one runs the risk of doing much harm. If the task set for me tends to dissipate me, it is something God does not wish for me, or it is a task that I do not know how to manage skillfully.

9. Have I not been tempted to consider calmness as a mere question of temperament, forgetting that temper can be moderated?

10. Have I observed in just what circumstances I lack serenity? Is it not specially when my self-love is touched, when my weak point is brought out into the open?

11. If I become unnerved, is it not at a time when I have undertaken too much, much more than I am able to

undertake? When I cannot accomplish the task, do I not become a victim of an inferiority complex?

12. Am I wont to view things and events from a supernatural point of view? Nothing so facilitates a return to calmness as to re-establish a sense of values and to consider things in the light of eternity, or at least as they may appear some years hence. In two or three years I shall have forgotten this untoward incident; in any case it will seem like a trifle and the jolt that I experience today will be singularly forgotten.

13. Whenever I deal with a soul do I make an effort to be not only calm but calming?

14. Many dissensions among men, among social classes, among nations, are a result of a fundamental misunderstanding of opposite points of view. Truth and justice are never completely on one side.
Can I not do a work to promote light and peace in many circumstances by explaining the sufferings and the legitimate desires of opposing factions? This calls for much tact and love. Ste Thérèse used to say: "It is not for us to be justices of peace, but angels of peace."

15. Have I understood the danger of allowing non-Christians the monopoly in the struggle for peace?
Have I not observed that there are many people led astray by false propaganda which represents the Church as having been allied with the munitions manufacturers and with those who agitate for war?

16. Am I capable of explaining what the Church has

done in the past and what she is doing continually to establish true peace?

17. Do I pray personally and do I recommend prayers for the reign of the peace of Christ, the fruit of justice and of love?

Resolutions

1. To communicate often that I may share in the peace of Christ and in the serenity and calmness which emanate from His Divine Person.

2. True peace is a gift of God. To pray for it humbly every day for myself, for others, for the whole world.

3. To become familiar with, to analyze, to assimilate the messages on peace published by the sovereign pontiff.

4. To make a note of and to meditate on the texts in the Mass which refer to peace.

5. Not to take too seriously the little difficulties inherent in every human group. To try to make little of the hurts, the misunderstandings, the oppositions that are inevitable. There is no opposition so complete that some point of agreement cannot be found. To make very evident these points of harmony, which very often are basic elements, before determining the points of discord which most of the time are merely problems in methods or in behavior. Then to try to solve both in an atmosphere of reconciliation. To invoke the Holy Spirit, asking Him to make clear the reasonable concessions which should be projected for the good of peace.

6. Never to reverse the plan of those of the opposition who make propositions. In the case of a growing antipathy, to make it a duty for myself to share the love of Christ with the one with whom I find myself involved; to think about his virtues; and to make an offering of them to the Lord, without forgetting to mention his "unknown virtues and merits"; to serve him in every way possible, and that with utmost kindness.

7. To remember that in the religious life God sometimes permits griefs annoying to self-love in order to give us occasion for humiliation and for meritorious pardon. Convents are rather like the Pasteur Institutes, veritable spiritual laboratories where the Lord comes to secure the serum of charity, of obedience, of peace, etc., in order to appropriate the fruits of the Redemption. They are more efficacious for the peace of the world than many sermons.

8. To beware of written messages. *Verba volant, scripta manent* ("Words fly away, written messages remain"). A word which is rather too sharp may escape us; it is easy to excuse it and to make reparation for it. But written words remain; and a bitter pen can inflict wounds which become infected.

Never to write when angry, and if I do so "to soothe my nerves," not to post my letter until the next day. In the meantime I should reread it calmly under the eye of God. Then I shall probably decide that I should write another, more gentle, and . . . more efficacious letter.

9. If lack of serenity is prominent in my character, I shall make use of autosuggestion. I shall imagine myself as I should be if I were perfectly calm, and I shall repeat peacefully: "I am calm, more and more calm . . ." and act accordingly.

10. If my lack of calmness and of serenity comes from a too crowded schedule, I shall proceed in an orderly way to make a list of my various tasks, indicating the order of their urgency, noting carefully the time needed for each of them. Then I shall watch that I do not trouble about the second task until I have finished the first calmly. To some one who wrote: "It is foolish to have as much work to do as I have: at least forty letters to answer!" A wise educator replied: "No, you have only one letter at a time to write. When you finish the first take the second, not before."

To plan how I can distribute some duties among my collaborators who could be called upon to do them. I should not try to do everything myself.

11. If my lack of tranquillity is a result of fatigue or of a passing indisposition, I should manage at any cost to get some rest periods, however short they be. To use the method of relaxing the muscles, and that of taking long and deep breaths.

12. If my lack of calmness comes from a tendency to give myself too exclusively to exterior things, then I will oblige myself to spend some few minutes in interior silence several times daily. To adore the Divine Host

in my soul, and to ask His blessing for the souls confided to my care.

13. If my lack of calmness comes from unexpected contradictions, I shall recall immediately that every such thing is a grace, and that each can be offered for the glory of God and the good of souls.

14. In the children for whom I am responsible, to develop a concern for others and the habit, so contrary to their egocentric instincts, of respecting the point of view of others. To teach them the art of reasonable concessions to others, and to encourage them to pardon others readily. "Do not let the sun go down upon your anger" (Eph. 4:26); "If thou art offering thy gift at the altar, and there rememberest that thy brother has anything against thee, leave thy gift before the altar and go first to be reconciled to thy brother, and then come and offer thy gift" (Matt. 5:23–24).

15. Not to hide from young people the fact that all men are not actuated by honest and disinterested motives, for they must not live in a dream world and later experience heartrending deceptions. To encourage them not to lose faith in the ideal of a better world. To make them see especially the whole picture, to draw their attention to the splendid examples of devotedness and of generosity which, through discretion, are often concealed, while hatreds and jealousies are paraded before the world.

16. In conversation, to avoid superficial criticisms and unfriendly ostracism of those of other social spheres

or of other races (Negroes, Jews, Arabs, etc.). To teach each child to view with interest the differences in the peoples who make up humanity, whom he will find picturesque and interesting when he knows how to regard them, how to think about them.[8]

17. To make known the *Pax Christi* Movement, a project to encourage prayer, thought, and action for peace, a movement highly recommended by the hierarchy.[9]

PRAYER

Heavenly Father, from whom comes every gift in this world, keep my soul ever in the peace which comes from You. Give me the grace never to be troubled by difficulties past, present, or future. Father, who love neither noise nor disturbance, grant that I may find in contemplation the calmness which I need so much to accomplish my tasks according to Your will and in Your Spirit. Father, You love union among Your children; grant, then, that harmony based on loyal inquiry of justice and charity may regulate my relations with my fellowmen for the greater good of all. Have pity on this poor world which seeks gropingly for peace and finds it not. May all men acknowledge Your Son and find with Your grace, in fundamental brotherhood, the secret of tasting the peace promised to men of good will.

AMEN

CHAPTER VIII

Confidence and Fear of God

The modern world is affected by a restlessness which develops in some people into a real neurosis. For some, life becomes an incomprehensible absurdity. It is as if behind closed doors they are turning round and round without knowing how to get out. They become confused to the point of nausea and end in despair. For others, life is a search for compensations under the guise of unbridled pleasures or a search for tasks which serve as evasions. For some, life is like the sword of Damocles, which represents a new world war more terrible than any in the past.

In a world so entangled, is it not our mission to inspire men with a reverential fear of God which leads to love and confidence?

Far too often, in the wake of the seventeenth century, God has been caricatured, presented as a tyrant lying in wait for human weakness; as an avenging God ready to casts thunderbolts upon men, rather than as the God of love, infinitely tender, indulgent, compassionate, who came to us not as a severe stranger but as a friend who, far from making us tremble, made Himself as the least of us, of whom no one could be afraid.

"When the goodness and kindness of God our Savior appeared, then not by reason of good works that we did ourselves, but according to his mercy, he saved us through the bath of regeneration and renewal by the Holy Spirit" (Tit. 3:4–5).

We shall have the opportunity of benefiting by this meditation on confidence.

Meditation

Let us adore our Lord presented by Mary to the shepherds. Let us listen to the angels as they bring us the message of peace and of joy: "A Savior has been born to you" (Luke 2:11). Let us hear our Lord's multiplied appeals for confidence: "It is not the healthy who need a physician, but they who are sick" (Luke 5:31); "I came that they may have life, and have it more abundantly" (John 10:10); "The Son of Man came to save what was lost" (Matt. 18:11); "For the Son of Man did not come to destroy men's lives, but to save them" (Luke 9:56). Let us note how many times He insists that they who approach Him should have no fear of Him: "Fear not." It is like a refrain repeated incessantly throughout the Gospel: "Have confidence!" "Peace be with you!" "It is I."

One of His last words is again an appeal for confidence: "Take courage, I have overcome the world" (John 16:33).

How could one fear Him who, at the very moment when His executioners nail His feet and hands to the Cross, asks His Father to pardon and pity them, for "they do not know what they are doing" (Luke 23:34), and promises paradise to the thief crucified beside Him? (Luke 23:43).

How can one fear a God who has made Himself so humble and little in the Sacred Host?

Let us study Him, His heart and arms opened wide as He calls us to Him: "Come to Me!" and waits for us to call Him to us. Let us say in the words of the Apocalypse: "Come, Lord Jesus!" (22:20).

Fear can serve as a guard-rail and at times as a barrier which prevents certain weak wills from abdicating, but it is not in itself a constructive force. Fear of chastisement can keep souls from danger, but if it is not supplemented by confidence and love, it leads to an emaciated outlook.

Fear, which is only fear, knows not how to honor God. A truly religious fear of God is rather confident respect than trembling.

Fear contracts, confidence dilates. Fear repels, confidence attracts. Fear creates the mentality of a hireling, confidence develops a childlike spirit. Fear makes one cowardly, confidence makes one courageous. Fear is content with the minimum required, confidence offers everything, although the Lord may be asking only a sample.

God wants us to go to Him and to lead souls to Him in complete confidence, for confidence is like the concentrated point of the three theological virtues.

Confidence is an act of faith, for it is a declaration that God exists and that God is to be depended upon by His creatures.

Confidence is an act of hope, for it depends upon the goodness and the mercy of God. God is not only One who calculates, but One on whom we can depend for all.

Confidence is an act of love, for the confident soul

forgets herself; she forgets her merits as well as her faults to think only of her Beloved, to give herself and to abandon herself to Him.

God does not like to see us disturbed about the past. Is not His power to pardon stronger than the power the whole world has to sin?

God does not like to see us disturbed about the present. In the most beautiful sense of the word, has He not made Himself our Companion on our way? Nothing that we do, nothing that we suffer escapes Him. Insofar as we wish it, He lives our life, He shares our suffering, He prays our prayers, He purifies, He sanctifies, He exalts.

God does not like to see us disturbed about the future. Let us recall the Gospel:

Therefore I say to you, do not be anxious for your life, what you shall eat; nor yet for your body, what you shall put on. Is not the life a greater thing than the food, and the body than the clothing? Look at the birds of the air: they do not sow, or reap, or gather into barns; yet your heavenly Father feeds them. Are not you of much more value than they? But which of you by being anxious about it can add to his stature a single cubit?

And as for clothing, why are you anxious? Consider how the lilies of the field grow; they neither toil nor spin, yet I say to you that not even Solomon in all his glory was arrayed like one of these. But if God so clothes the grass of the field, which flourishes today but tomorrow is thrown into the oven, how much more you, O you of little faith!

Therefore do not be anxious saying, "What shall we eat?" or, "What shall we drink?" or, "What are we to put on?" (for after all these things the Gentiles seek); for your Father knows that you need all these things. But seek first the kingdom of God and his justice, and all these things shall be given you besides. Therefore do not be anxious about tomorrow; for tomorrow will have anxieties of its own. Sufficient for the day is its own trouble (Matt. 6:25–34).

Let us meditate on some texts about confidence found in Holy Scripture. Let us note in the Psalms all the benefits of confidence, especially the well-known verses of Psalm 90:

He that dwelleth in the aid of the most High, shall abide under the protection of the God of Heaven.

He shall say to the Lord: Thou art my protector and my refuge: my God, in him will I trust.

For he hath delivered me from the snare of the hunters: and from the sharp word.

He will overshadow thee with his shoulders: and under his wings thou shalt trust.

His truth shall compass thee with a shield: thou shalt not be afraid of the terror of the night.

Of the arrow that flieth in the day, of the business that walketh about in the dark: of invasion, or of the noonday devil. . . .

Because thou, O Lord, art my hope: thou hast made the most High thy refuge.

There shall no evil come to thee: nor shall the scourge come near thy dwelling.

For he hath given his angels charge over thee, to keep thee in all thy ways (1–6, 9–11).

They that trust in the Lord shall be as Mount Sion: he shall not be moved for ever that dwelleth in Jerusalem (Ps. 124:1).

The Lord is my helper: I will not fear what man can do unto me.

The Lord is my helper: and I will look over his enemies.

It is good to confide in the Lord, rather than to have confidence in man. . . .

The Lord is my strength and my praise: and he is become my salvation (Ps. 117:6–8, 14).

Let us stir up our memories: have we not had the experience that when in all humility we have confided all our concerns to the Divine Master, everything turns out for our greater good?

"We should place our hope in God," said Péguy, "for He has placed His hope in us!"

Colloquy

My daughter, too often I am disappointed in religious souls when I do not find in them the confidence I should expect from them.

Paradoxically, they believe in Me and yet they doubt Me.

They believe in My existence, they believe in My power, they believe in My love, but in a conceptual, a speculative, a theoretical way. Practically, they doubt My continual presence, they doubt My merciful goodness, they doubt My affectionate and tender interest in them, they doubt My ardent desire to live their life, to unite them to Me, to make all their activities fruitful. It is thus that they destroy My effectiveness.

The fear in some religious souls stifles me. The confidence in some religious souls gives Me freedom and permits Me to act in them.

Why do you not have more confidence in Me? What stops you?

My greatness? . . . Consider how far I went to make Myself little, humble, considerate. Contemplate the crib, the cross, the Sacred Host. Look at Me living so simply at Nazareth, at Cana, at Capharnaum, at Bethany.

My Divinity? . . . Think of how far I made Myself a part of humanity. I became completely a man among men, so that I was not a stranger nor indifferent to anything that is human.

My power? . . . It is entirely at your service. If you have faith there is nothing that you cannot obtain. I make use of My power only through love.

My demands? . . . They have no other end but to improve all the hidden riches which I have placed in your soul, to give to your religious life complete fruitfulness, to win for you the greatest amount of happiness and of glory for eternity. Moreover I am in you to help you to cooperate. I am always at hand when you call Me, ready, if you permit Me, to fill you with divine strength.

My Cross? . . . If any one wishes to be My disciple, most certainly he must take up his cross. My Mother, whom I love more tenderly than the most loving of sons, has not been spared the cross. But, first of all, I proportion the cross to the shoulders of each one, and then, am I not at hand to help carry each cross? I have experience, you need not fear. Then the cross, far from crushing you, raises you up and gives you power to draw souls to Me.

What is it that makes you hesitate? Perhaps they are your many sins, your many meannesses, your many negligences? Yes, you are right: You can never regret them too much. But if you have asked My pardon humbly, you know well that they are given over to My mercy. Your faults, once absolved, are completely forgotten in My heart. If I leave you the memory of them, it is not to discourage you, nor to keep your soul disturbed, but to keep you in humility, to make you more prudent, and to stir up your charity for others.

The fear of judgment? . . . You will be judged according to your love and *by* Love. Do you think that I can forget all that you have done for Me? I forget the faults, but I do not forget the proofs of love that you have given Me so often during life, beginning with your response to My appeal, when at your profession you gave Me your soul and body, your whole being. Nor do I forget all the acts of love which you have forgotten long since. To be sure, all that is in obscurity here below, for it is the duty of love to safeguard your humility. But it is a duty very dear to My heart to keep an account of all your generous responses to My appeals. May they be more and more numerous in the details of your daily life, for nothing done through love is small!

My daughter, be not timid with Me! Since I call you, come! Since I love you, love! There is nothing about Me to frighten you. Under My eye be confident, silent, firm. If there is anything to repair, I repair it. If there is anything to cure, I cure it. If there is anything to supply, I supply it.

Your whole life is very precious to Me. There is nothing in you to prevent you from serving Me by helping some soul in distress, far away and unknown. If only you knew the value and the power of a consecrated life! . . .

When I see on this earth a soul which is completely confident of My love and which abandons itself without fear into My hands, I can refuse that soul nothing. I would not want that soul to be disappointed for anything in the world. But alas! such souls are very rare . . .

Has not the Psalmist declared: "The Lord ruleth me: and I shall want nothing" (22:1)? Have you not had experience of that? How many times I have intervened in your behalf, and I would do it much more often if you would do Me the honor of relying on Me a little more in every circumstance.

It is as God that I keep My promises. It is as God that I make suitable return for your humble and loyal confidence. You honor Me more by the confidence that you place in Me than by anything else that you can do for Me.

Examen

1. What is the habitual condition of my spiritual life? Discouragement, anxiety, deception, bitterness, sharpness, inertness, more occupied with what is disappointing than with what goes well? Or is it thanksgiving, a realistic and positive view of people, things, events, a courageous confidence and a filial abandonment into the hands of God?

2. Have I understood thoroughly all the harm that can be done in a community of souls who, according to La Tour du Pin, *"let hope perish"*?

3. Should I not make a complete survey of my con-

fidence in God, both in my apostolic life and in my spiritual life?

4. Have I not had proof that the grace infused in baptism into the souls of my pupils was not in vain? Should I not appeal to it more often?

5. Why is it that I am so often fearful, timid, constrained with our Lord? Should I not be much more simple in my relations with Him?

6. Have I understood fully all the harm that a discouraged teacher can do in the apostolate? Is not discouragement often the fruit of deceived pride? Does it not originate in the practical forgetfulness of the primary role of God, without whom we can do nothing?

7. Do I firmly believe that nothing that is done through love is lost, and that all the little acts—obscure but generous—accomplished in union with Christ, have more efficacy for the salvation of the world than deeds done with a flourish or apparent successes contrived by pride?

8. In my community am I a sower of optimism and of confidence?

9. Am I wise enough to avoid presumption, which is only a false confidence in one's rights and in one's talents, while Christian confidence has a twofold foundation: the wretchedness of man and the mercy of God?

Resolutions

1. To ask God often for a better understanding of the virtue of hope, and for an increase of it in my soul.

2. Never to yield to discouragement. To keep in mind that of all solutions this is the most undesirable.

3. To meditate often on reasons for confidence in God.

4. To note all the texts which, in Holy Scripture and in the liturgy, express confidence or make an appeal for it.

5. From time to time, to enumerate all the delicate marks of kindness received from Divine Providence throughout my life. Those which we have not noticed are more numerous still.

6. To look upon a lack of confidence toward our Lord as an injustice, an injury, an act of ingratitude.

Reading [1]

Many men have learned in their childhood to avoid evil rather than to do good; to fear chastisements rather than to devote themselves in love to the love of God. They have been taught about death, about the dangers of this life; they have been told so little of the joy of living, and of the glory of being united with God here—the only requirement for birth into eternity. They have been taught to watch for the pitfalls which endanger their every step. They have not been shown the heights which call to them above the valleys enveloped in darkness, heights which are the resting place of the Sun.

Then, tired of repelling the impulses which they knew not how to regulate, they have rushed in all directions wherever their flight met no barriers. And they have had, at least for some time, the impression that they were living.

Many since then have been turned against their teachers and have become hostile to a religion which seemed to them to measure out in small drops the right to think, to know, and to love, at the same time to envelop all their movements in that suspicion which forbids the most beautiful things they might enjoy.

Nothing is more contrary to the true spirit of Christianity, however, than this drying up process which only too often ends in a religious pedagogy so applied as to present negatively a doctrine which is above all essentially vital.

. . . Most men are not so corrupted that they remain insensible to love; it is not often that they resist disinterested goodness. The goodness of God is primarily disinterested. Would more men not have been attracted by God's love if their hearts had not been suspicious of infernal abysses? Many, I believe, have looked upon their Creator as a rival rather than a friend. Many have seemed to revolt because they could not reconcile the desire for expansion inherent in their nature with the suppression proposed to them in the name of virtue.

. . . The Commandments of God do not purpose to break our nature, which is God's work, but to insure harmony in all our faculties through a divine realization of all our instincts.

If these instincts are insatiable in their disorder, they are at the same time infinite in their vocation; the degree of abjection to which they can descend reveals the degree of the height to which they are called.

PRAYER

Lord Jesus, you ask from all souls whom you have chosen through love a complete confidence and a total abandonment. Give me, then, the grace never to disappoint You. I give myself to You without reserve. Tell me what You wish me to think, what You wish me to say, what You wish me to do. In every circumstance may I follow Your way, the way that You have traced out for me, for the Way is You, and You are Love.

AMEN

CHAPTER IX

The Sacred Host and Our Religious Life

It is our privilege—one of the greatest privileges of our religious life—to spend time daily before the tabernacle and from time to time before the exposed Blessed Sacrament.

Every such occasion is "An Hour with Jesus" *par excellence,* the hour for which He pleaded with His apostles and concerning which there have been revelations, like that of Paray-le-Monial, declared authentic by the Church.

In the presence of the Sacred Host, the religious soul expands like the flowers before the sun and imbibes the divine energy necessary for her supernatural task. In the presence of the Sacred Host, the religious soul becomes more conscious of the true character of her vocation, which consists in a constant oblation immersed in that of Christ Jesus, as the drop of water is combined with the wine in the chalice. In the presence of the Sacred Host, the religious soul learns precious lessons about the virtues which should be hers at the same time that she absorbs the strength to be faithful.

Should we not add here that in the presence of the Sacred Host the religious teacher finds again all the souls which have been confided to her, so that she may present them to Him who alone can help them efficaciously?

How many reasons there are to orient our prayer toward Eucharistic contemplation!

Meditation

Let us adore Jesus really present in the Sacred Host. Let us make an act of faith in His divine presence.

The Master is there and He calls to us. . . . It is He who has the words of eternal life. . . . To whom shall we go, O Lord? . . . You are the Light of the World. . . . Who follows You walks not in darkness. . . . You are the Sun of Justice. . . . From You go forth rays which can cure all of us. . . . You are the center of all hearts. . . . In You we are reunited with all our brothers, even those who are already in the house of the Father. . . . You are a burning furnace of charity. . . . It is in You, with You, and by You that we render to the Father, in the unity of the Holy Spirit, all honor and glory.

Let us try now to study the riches and the lessons of the Holy Eucharist as a help to our religious and apostolic life.

The Blessed Sacrament is a mystery, *The Mystery of Faith,* to quote the words of Consecration at Holy Mass. "Mystery" here does not mean, as is too often believed, a reality contrary to reason, nor even a totally inaccessible truth, but a truth so precious that it is fathomless, that it is possible always to discover something new in it. The more acute is the eye of faith—and it is prolonged contemplation that makes it such—the more wonders are revealed. Gradually they reveal more and more splendors.

The Sacred Host is a mystery of hope. Hope is a hunger for God. If Jesus gives Himself to us under the "appearance" of a piece of bread, it is to remind us that He wishes to be for our souls what bread is for the body, according to the words of St. Ambrose: "the constant remedy of our incessant misery." For this end it is necessary that there increase in us:

—the sense of our misery: let us repeat *Kyrie eleison* . . . "Lord, I am not worthy . . ."

—the sense of the need that we have of God: "Without me you can do nothing" (John 15:5).

—the sense of confidence in His power: "I can do all things in him who strengthens me" (Phil. 4:13).

—the appetite and the relish for God: The more a soul is nourished with God, the more there grows in her the desire to receive Him. As St. Gregory Nazianzen says: "God hungers for us to hunger for Him."

The Sacred Host is likewise a mystery of hope, for as we sing in the *O sacrum convivium,* it is in the Host that we are given the pledge and the beginning of life eternal. "Life eternal," said St. Augustine, "is to possess God and to be possessed by Him in the fullness of light." The Eucharistic life is that mutual possession on earth, but in darkness.

The Sacred Host is a mystery of love. To love is not only to give, but to give oneself completely. There is no greater proof of love than to give one's life for the beloved. When our Lord declares His presence, He assures us that at the same time He gives Himself: "This is my body, which is being given for you" (Luke 22 : 19). Can one conceive a gift more complete, more dispossessed, more permanent than that of the Sacred Host?

The Lord gives Himself to us without reserve, without measure, without ever reclaiming His gift. He gives us not only His teaching, His example, His virtues, His merits, His consolations, His powers, but His body, His blood, His soul, and the fullness of His Divinity. We can profit by all these in proportion to our receptivity, which it depends on us to increase.

We need never fear that we shall exhaust all these gifts, for He is Infinite Love—that is to say, infinitely more tender, more powerful, more ardent, more strong, more compassionate than we can ever imagine. Human adjectives are poor stammerings beside the dazzling reality.

The Sacred Host is a mystery of union. "Love strains with all its might," according to St. Augustine, "for embrace, for blending, for union."

The Host is a mystery of union of the soul with God. According to the measure of our interior embrace of Him, there results an exchange of all that we are and of all that He is, so that we realize the better the words of St. Paul: "It is now no longer I that live, but Christ lives in me" (Gal. 2 : 20).

That this exchange be possible, there must be a true gift of our complete self to Him. Most certainly our religious life is a substantial offering, and that is why the religious soul is so united with the Holy Eucharist. But it is not sufficient that the gift be made once for all: it is necessary to make this initial gift, the gift of our *yes* in answer to the divine call, a gift which we made official on the day of our Profession, actual in the daily oblation of all the small and great happenings of our lives. That a gift be valid it is not necessary that it be made with our heart's blood, but when the gift does entail suffering we give a sure proof that our love is not an illusion.

A religious who has understood the sense of the Eucharistic life is not surprised to have a share in the Joyful Mysteries and to have happy hours; nor is she any more surprised to have a share in the Sorrowful Mysteries and to have to offer fatigue, afflictions, sacrifices, painful obedience, unjust and unexpected humiliations. It is no trifling thing that she offers to God, so that He may apply His mercy. She says with the Secret of the Mass of Wednesday of the Second Week of Lent: "By this holy exchange loosen, O Lord, the bonds of our sins . . ."

The Sacred Host is also a mystery of union of all men among themselves. Let us recall the symbolism that the Fathers of the Church loved to see even in the making of bread, and which the famous hymn sums up: "As the grains of pure wheat are blended in the Host, so the grains of pure wheat have united our souls."

At the moment of the Institution of the Holy Eucharist, Jesus solemnly proclaimed what He called His Commandment: "A new commandment I give you, that you love one another: that as I have loved you, you also love one another" (John 13:34). He summed up the most ardent wish of His Heart in this gemlike formula: "That all may be one, even as thou, Father, in me and I in thee" (John 17:21).

Insistently He repeats it: "That they may be one even

as we are one: I in them and thou in me; that they may be perfected in unity" (John 27:22–23).

The Sacred Host is there to remind us that Jesus is the center of every community, as He is the center of all humanity. We are in Him and He is in us. He is in the innermost part of our souls and we are deep in His Sacred Heart. Not only do we believe that all are united in Him, and He in all, but that He is in each one and each one in Him.

He is, as Gaston de Renty said, "the divine cement of unity"; yet more: He is the vital influx which unites us interiorly. Every conflict among us is for Him acute suffering. He feels as if we are tearing His body apart. The offering made by a soul who harbors resentment against another loses in His eyes all value; worse still, that soul, by its hardness, becomes a stranger in the oblation of the mystery of unity.

This is borne out by the words of Jesus: "Therefore, if thou art offering thy gift at the altar, and there rememberest that thy brother has anything against thee, leave thy gift before the altar and go first to be reconciled to thy brother, and then come and offer thy gift" (Matt. 5:23–24).

If we take the Gospel a bit more literally, we shall be careful each day to purify our hearts from all harshness, from all bitterness. Then we shall try in the spirit of the Holy Eucharist, by our desire for peace, to be the leaven of unity for all around us.

Colloquy

My daughter, it is in the Sacred Host that you can meditate on the ideal of your religious life. Look at the Host most earnestly, so that you will see all the power of love that I have put into your heart. Then you will understand a little better what you must try to become.

Like the consecrated Host, you must be a soul consecrated to the glory of the Father, to the interests of the Father, to the will of the Father.

Through the words of Consecration the entire substance of the bread has become the substance of My body. Only the appearances of bread are left, under which I hide Myself, I live, I think, I pray, I devote Myself. But in very truth *I* am there.

The substance offers no resistance to its transubstantiation. Only five words are needed to perform the miracle.

Because you are a personality endowed with freedom, you have the power to resist or to comply. Let your whole life on this earth comply loyally and completely with Me. Your personality need never disappear, but what can and ought to disappear is, insofar as you will it, anything that would be an obstacle to the blending of your will with Mine.

Interiorly, a religious is a soul that, like the Sacred Host, is entirely penetrated with Me. Exteriorly, one can distinguish no difference between a consecrated Host and a host that has not been consecrated. But in the eyes of faith as in those of the Eternal Father, what a difference! For you, too, it is the interior that counts in the sight of the Father. He wants to recognize in you the sentiments the dispositions, the virtues of His Son. He would like to find Me in you. For that reason let Me make use of you to pray to My Father by your prayer, to give Myself to souls by your devotedness; let Me continue through you My life of oblation, of poverty, of purity, of obedience, of charity, of silence.

With one quick movement I can produce from bread the Eucharistic Species, so as to nourish all men sacramentally and to unite them in charity. With you, it is only bit by bit, according as you live your offering, that I can make use of your humanity to make My presence felt in souls, that I can dispense through you My light, and My power, and My peace.

Have you given thought to this? Before I instituted the Holy Eucharist I pronounced these words: "I have given you an example, that as I have done to you, so you also should do" (John 13:15).

In the Sacred Host are there not substantial evidences of the religious virtues which you ought to practice? For example, when you look toward the tabernacle is it not My love of silence that impresses you? I could have done otherwise, but I have chosen a method which requires complete silence. I, the Word, the substantial Word of the Father, the Master of Truth, I teach in silence and I must be heard in silence. How rare are the souls who know how to reserve zones of silence in order to be on the alert for My words to them! Beg the grace to know how to be silent so that you can hear Me better, and that you may make more efficacious the words that you will say.

Poverty? Humility? See how simple is the raw material of the Eucharist: a little bread, a little wine, almost nothing. See how far I have extended My humility. I love poor means. And you, you should not rely on human resources, on special inventions, nor on your talents, nor on your relations in order to do the work of My Father. Love the means that I took to gain souls and to save the world: the hidden life, humble work, prayer, sacrifice, the slow formation—sometimes deceiving—of a group of rough men to whom I communicated My love and My zeal.

Obedience? Is not the Eucharist the acme of obedience? Whenever a priest pronounces the words of Consecration with the intention of doing what the Church intends, as soon as those words are pronounced I am present there, truly committed to his hands.

You, too, should be docile to the commands of your Superior. Only one thing is necessary: to do the will of My Father. You are never more sure of fulfilling His Divine Will than when you are where obedience assigns you.

Purity? Chastity? The Sacred Host is immaculate, and am I not an antidote and a remedy for all malignant fevers? The delicacy of your conscience, the purity of your intentions, the mortification of your body make of you a soul whose very presence—and even whose memory— purifies, sustains, and spiritualizes all souls who approach you.

Charity? Is not the Sacred Host the supreme gift, the undeniable proof of the love that transcends human limitations: love that gives itself to be the food of the beloved? Can there be a more complete gift of self than this, and a gift given not just once in the history of the world, but every day, millions of times a day?

You, you ought to be a soul consumed by all the cares of others, across every circumstance of which are inscribed my designs of love. But do not forget this: you should be so intimately united with Me that in giving yourself you really give Me.

Have confidence, my daughter. No life is more fruitful than yours if your life is truly the life of the Host with its continual immolation.

Examen

1. Have I sufficient faith in the Real Presence of Jesus in the Sacred Host? Has my faith not rather become routine? Should I not try to make it more living, more intelligent, more practical?

2. Have I a real hunger for Jesus in the Blessed Sacrament? Is Holy Mass truly the center of my religious life, which is essentially a life of oblation in communion with the Divine Victim, so that I may apply the fruits of the Redemption for the spiritual profit of the souls in my care?

3. Do I give sufficient time to thanksgiving, profiting by the moments when I possess corporeally Him in whom resides the plenitude of Divinity? Do I aim at the maximum of virtues and at a total union with our Lord, and through Him with the Church, all of this with a view to sanctifying the day ahead?

4. Whenever I have an occasion do I love to kneel be-

fore the tabernacle and profit by the graces which emanate from Jesus in the Holy Eucharist? Let us recall the Gospel texts: "Power went forth from him and healed all" (Luke 6:19); "Someone touched me, for I perceived that power had gone forth from me" (Luke 8:46).

5. Am I watchful to give to the children under my care a solid Eucharistic formation, instilling into them a profound respect for the Blessed Sacrament?

6. Am I convinced that this formation is one of the most efficacious means, not only to safeguard their fidelity, but to develop in them a sense of Christian unity and of fraternal charity?

7. Is the Mass for me a participation, in union with the Church, in the oblation of Christ actually on the altar? What should be the consequences which will help me to live the Mass more seriously and to make it understood better by the young people confided to my care?

Resolutions

1. To make the Holy Eucharist more truly the center of my spiritual and apostolic life.

2. To try to live in a state of oblation to the Father, in union with Jesus in the Sacred Host, and for the benefit of the Church.

3. To deepen in my own soul and to give to my pupils a great respect for the Real Presence, and for all that concerns the Blessed Sacrament.

4. To teach children to prepare for Holy Communion, without, however, asking them to do anything beyond their strength. To show them how everything can be a part of that preparation, in particular the loving accomplishment of each duty assigned to them, generous obedience at home, little services performed, efforts to improve their characters, etc.

5. To explain to children the spirit of offering, the offering of themselves, the offering of others, particularly of those who are suffering, in union with Jesus our Eucharistic Lord. To explain to them the meaning of the Redemption of the world. To show them how, by Holy Communion, they can be connecting links between Jesus and souls.

6. To teach them to make thanksgiving personal, which does not mean individualistic. To insist on the communal character of Holy Mass and of Holy Communion.

For this purpose to use the formula *"Ardor"*:

A: .... *A*dore
R: .... *R*eturn Thanks
D: .... *D*esire Graces
O: .... *O*ffer
R: .... *R*esolve

To suggest that they keep a notebook of personal intentions in which a large part will be devoted to the great intentions of Holy Church. To be watchful so they may have at least a few minutes of silent prayer after Holy Mass. If possible, to conclude with a prayer said in common, and not to make an unwise use of repeated *Paters* and *Aves*.

7. To give them a love for visits to the Blessed Sacrament. To make visits together from time to time, visits that have been prepared carefully and that are conducted intelligently, always allowing some time for silent prayer. To suggest to them, particularly if it is convenient for them, to go to a church on their way home from school, and so cultivate the habit of personal visits to the Blessed Sacrament.

8. To teach them the method of spiritual Communion, which is the best preparation for sacramental Communion. To put them on their guard against human respect lest it prevent them from communicating or make them communicate because others do so. It is of the greatest importance that the approach of children to Jesus be spontaneous and voluntary.

PRAYER

Dear Lord Jesus, make me understand better the spirit of oblation which should characterize my religious and apostolic life. I offer myself generously to You, that it may be You I give them when I give myself. Without You, Jesus, I can do nothing, but with You there is nothing I cannot do. Teach me to live more united with You and with my Sisters. I give myself to You without reserve so that You may make use of me freely for all the tasks You wish of me. Grant that, following the example of Mary, I may become a ray of Your divine charity.

AMEN

CHAPTER X

A Sense of Eternity

Many of our contemporaries are swept away in a whirlwind of business, of wealth, or of sensual pleasures. Noise, ever more deafening; speed, endless and ever increasing, wears them out. As Holy Scripture says: "They do not take time to breathe."

How can they find God when they cannot find themselves? How can they view things in the light of eternity when time is for them an implacable tyrant which devours their thinking and absorbs their energy?

Sometimes, as on the Feast of All Saints or at the death of a dear one, they do give a furtive thought to the great beyond. But other problems soon claim their renewed interest. Moreover, they take the attitude that death is only for others. As Xavier de Maistre said: "Others may die, that is to be understood; does he not see that happening every day? But that he might die himself, that is beyond understanding."

Young people say: "There is plenty of time to think!" In Ronsard's *Ode to Cassandra* it is the same pagan theme:

> . . . Whilst your life is crowned
> With its springlike beauty,
> Enjoy, enjoy your youth. . . .

The aged, immersed in their memories, think only of the past and turn away from thoughts of death, often so near to them. An ostrich-like prudence!

Our earthly life, however, makes sense only when it is viewed as a preparation for eternity. To close one's eyes to the great beyond; to refuse to concentrate on the life that will never end; to center one's thoughts on the life that will be over some day, is an absurdity. And yet this thoughtless attitude is so widespread!

In a moment of unexpected lucidity, the son of Dumas wrote: "If one wishes to have a correct view of things of this life, I believe that he should think very often of death."

Is it not a duty for Christian educators to give to young people an awareness of eternity, which alone enables them to recognize true fundamental values and to renounce base considerations? How necessary it is for teachers to develop this discernment in themselves that they may throw light on what would otherwise mislead their pupils.

Meditation

Let us begin by adoring Jesus, who made incessant allusions to eternal life. Let us gather some of these references and meditate on them.

"My kingdom is not of this world" (John 18:36); "What does it profit a man if he gain the whole world but ruin or lose himself?" (Luke 9:25); "Come, blessed of my Father, take possession of the kingdom prepared for you from the foundation of the world" (Matt. 25:34); "Blessed are the poor in spirit, for theirs is the kingdom of heaven" (Matt. 5:3); "The kingdom of God is at hand. Repent and believe in the Gospel" (Mark 1:15); "Whoever humbles himself as this little child, he is the greatest in the kingdom of heaven" (Matt. 18:4); "Those who believe in Christ will not perish, but will have life everlasting" (John 3:15); "Your reward is great in heaven" (Matt. 5:12).

Reread the parable of the rich man and Lazarus:

There was a certain rich man who used to clothe himself in purple and fine linen, and who feasted every day in splendid fashion. And there was a certain poor man, named Lazarus, who lay at his gate, covered with sores, and longing to be filled with the crumbs that fell from the rich man's table; even the dogs would come and lick his sores. And it came to pass that the poor man died and was borne away by the angels into Abraham's bosom; but the rich man also died and was buried in hell (Luke 16:19–22).

And that of the rich farmer:

The land of a certain rich man brought forth abundant crops. And he began to take thought within himself, saying, "What shall I do, for I have no room to store my crops?" And he said, "I will do this: I will pull down my barns and build larger ones, and there I will store up all my grain and my goods. And I will say to my soul, Soul, thou hast many good things laid up for many years; take thy ease, eat, drink, be merry." But God said to him, "Thou fool, this night do they demand thy soul of thee; and the things that thou hast provided, whose will they be?" So is he who lays up treasure for himself, and is not rich as regards God (Luke 12:16–21).

St. Paul never ceases drawing the attention of Christians to the life which will never end:

Here we have no permanent city, but we seek for the city that is to come (Heb. 13:14).

For our present light affliction, which is for the moment, prepares for us an eternal weight of glory that is beyond all measure; while we look not at the things that are seen, but at the things that are not seen. For the things that are seen are temporal, but the things that are not seen are eternal (2 Cor. 4:17–18).

For we know that if the earthly house in which we dwell be destroyed, we have a building from God, a house not made by human hands, eternal in the heavens. And indeed, in this present state we groan, yearning to be clothed over with that dwelling of ours which is from heaven; if indeed we shall be found clothed, and not naked. For we who are in this tent sigh under our burden, because we do not wish to be unclothed, but rather clothed over, that what is mortal may be swallowed up by life. Now he who made us for this very thing is God, who has given us the Spirit as its pledge.

Always full of courage, then, and knowing that while we are in the body we are exiled from the Lord—for we walk by faith and not by sight—we even have the courage to prefer to be exiled from the body and to be at home with the Lord (2 Cor. 5:1–8).

The Bible multiplies the reminders of the shortness of life: "Man's days are as grass: as the flower of the field so shall he flourish" (Ps. 102:15).

How many times the expression "eternal life" recurs in our prayers! Why does it evoke so little response in us?

No one is sure of another day. The Lord reminds us of our duty to be ready at any instant for our departure from this life: "Watch therefore, for you know neither the day nor the hour" (Matt. 25:13); "I will come upon thee as a thief" (Apoc. 3:3).

As one advances in life, the years seem to pass more quickly. But, paradoxically, it seems easier to die when one is young than when one is old.

In reality our eternity has commenced: we are in the earthly phase of our existence. How brief this phase is compared to that which will never end! This earthly life, however, is very important, since on this short period our state and our degree of glory for all eternity will depend!

To live with our thoughts on eternity is not to desert the earth nor to neglect our duty here, but to inject into our thoughts of death the strength to live with more intensity in the present by penetrating our life with God, and by offering it to Him.

The first Christians called the day of their death *dies natalis:* "Birthday," the day of their birth into eternal life.

For us the next life is a mystery, that is to say a fathomless reality, but a reality which envelops us on all sides. Many men ask how they can communicate with those who have passed through the curtain of the realm of darkness. Have we not the Lord Jesus Himself, who, in the Sacred Host, is always with us in this life at the same time that He is in eternity?

Death is only a word, a passage, our Easter. In truth, if our life changes its mode by death, it is not taken away. *Vita mutatur, non tollitur:* "Life is changed, not taken away" (Preface of the Mass for the Dead). On the contrary, it is expanded in the possession of the Light; better still, in the possession of Him who is the Light, who will share with us, without shadow and without change, the knowledge of what He is, the love of what He loves, the joy that He experiences.

After the necessary purifications which will have our full compliance—a compliance which engenders a supreme hope—we shall be completely penetrated by Him as the coal is penetrated by fire. And as the coal becomes fire itself without ceasing to be coal, so shall we become absorbed in God without ceasing to be ourselves.

"Eye has not seen nor ear heard, nor has it entered into the heart of man, what things God has prepared for those who love him" (1 Cor. 2:9).

Whatever we can imagine as most beautiful, most inspiring, most unexpected, is nothing compared with the great realities which we shall experience. This entrance into the joy of the Lord will be dazzling, a life lived in an incessantly renewed burst of happiness, to which nothing on earth can be compared. It is better to adore and to be silent. But one understands how St. Paul, who was superlatively zealous to save souls, could, after having been granted special divine secrets, cry out in faith and in love: "I desire to depart and to be with Christ" (Phil. 1:23); "For me . . . to die is gain" (Phil. 1:21).

Colloquy

Because I have a great respect for your free will as long as you are on earth, I shall be for you a hidden God, and I shall conceal from your eyes the wonders that await you. For I have created you for the life beyond, for a life which will be final. Even though you may be nothing and capable of nothing, I have extended My tenderness for you so as to will that with My love you may be rich in merits, so that you may enjoy deserved happiness.

That explains My dealing with you here on earth. If I were but completely understood . . . !

My daughter, live each hour as the most beautiful of your life, because each hour—with its particular tonality, its special color, its unique place in the history of the time —has an eternal import.

If you but knew the attention I give to your desires and to your secret intentions! If you but knew the price I put on the movements of your heart! If you but knew the value I set on the least of your efforts! If you but knew the power you can exercise by your faith, your confidence, your love, in the invisible realm of souls!

Put Me into your life more—that is, into your thinking, into your preoccupations, into your plans, into your work. For that reason, live in a spirit of oblation. It is the best apprenticeship and the best preparation for your future life. The more you offer to Me, the more I can become a part of you here below in obscurity—later and forever, in full light. Your life, your whole life, is what I want.

You see, heaven is the desire for Me and the eternal possession of Me. Damnation is to turn from Me always, to drive Me away unceasingly. What an appalling thing! To repel Love deliberately, light, joy—and this through pride: *Non serviam!* ("I will not serve!").

I appreciate so much the free-will offerings of themselves which men make to Me, that while bestowing generously on them help, light, and other proofs of My love (what could I do more for them: My Incarnation, My Passion, My Mother, My Church, My sacraments, the example of My saints, the sufferings of My martyrs, the zeal of My apostles . . .), I will never violate the freedom of their wills. It is most painful to see myself repulsed by men when I love them so much!

If you could see things as I view them and as you will see them some day, you would not be astonished at the trials that I permit in your life. Difficulties, obstacles, contradictions, discomforts, and illnesses, all these crosses, all these thorns, are part of the background which must be yours in this life. They establish the pledge of great rewards which will astonish you, for the least proof of love will redound in glory for you.

A saint has not been a saint always. But My grace has

not been lacking, and the saintly soul has corresponded in humility and in generosity. I do not ask you to be an angel, but to be a saint according to your nature, according to your graces, in the surroundings wherein I have placed you. Be not anxious: nothing that concerns you escapes Me. Yours is the type of life suitable for the task which I have assigned to you. I send you crosses to fit the shoulders I have given to you.

As long as you are on this earth give Me meritorious faith, meritorious charity, meritorious obedience. You will not be able to give them to Me in heaven, and I need them so much for so many souls.

When you will be in eternity you will look at things far differently. You will think only of your progress in love, and you will realize that each day of your earthly pilgrimage gave you an opportunity to help and to save many thousands of souls.

Think more often of the joys of heaven. They will help you to be happy in the midst of the sadness of this world. Do you know that every day, through My Church, the saint whose feast is kept has graces to give to those on earth, if we but ask for them?

In eternity you will say to yourself: How could I have let an hour pass without showing my love for Him? Accustom yourself to make eternity your goal. Nothing is of importance unless it has some bearing on that end.

One must be very humble to enter heaven. When you see Me you will understand that there is nothing worse than pride. Who is as pure as God? Who is as humble as He is? In this world there are only sinners, those who have been preserved from sin, and those who have been purified. Woe to those who are proud that they have not yielded to temptations which they never experienced!

Let not the thought of death frighten you. It will be the day of the great meeting, the eternal meeting. And it will be at the same time a precious occasion to give Me the greatest proof of love. Be happy to think that some day you will die of love for Me, since I have died for love of you.

Think often of the home that will be yours in heaven. Far from distracting you from your present duty, the thought of eternity will but give it greater meaning and more importance. Far from making you a self-seeker, the thought of eternity will make you discover the value of forgetfulness of self for the good of others, since, after all, time has been given to you only to exercise and to increase your love.

Examen

1. Do I not all too often judge and act according to human views?

2. Why do I have so many difficulties to beset my bond with eternity through faith?

3. Do I understand that the most important realities are eternal?

4. Have I not fallen into the opposite excess, refusing to integrate human values in the synthesis of the divine plan, forgetting that the law of the Incarnation is not so much the insertion of the divine into the human as the assumption of the human by the divine?

5. Am I not of those mentioned by Péguy, who say that they are not interested in the world under the pretext that they are very specially endowed by grace?

6. Am I accustomed to look into every problem to find out what relation it bears to eternity?

7. Am I not inclined to be concerned only about what is my personal problem, forgetting that I am a unit in a great ensemble which is called the Church and that I am marching toward the kingdom? Or, if one prefers it: I am a member of the Mystical body of Christ Jesus, each cell predestined to share His glory eternally.

8. Is my belief clear concerning the resurrection of the body? Do I think often of the great moment of the meeting, of that great meeting in heaven? What are the thoughts which predominate in me when I think of death: indifference, forlornness, fear, anxiety? or confidence, desire, joy, enthusiasm?

9. Am I truly convinced that there is only a slight barrier between me and death?

Resolutions

1. To ask our Lord every day to develop in me a Christian attitude toward death and an awareness of eternity.

2. To establish a true scale of values from the point of view of eternity.

3. To consider the years here below as the terrestrial

phase of a life whose circumstances will be changed by death, but whose fundamental character will endure.

4. To appreciate at their just value the years of life which remain to me, the only ones in which I can merit; later, it will be eternally too late to merit.

5. To establish more and more relations of prayer, of mutual help, and of friendship with the suffering and with the triumphant members of the Mystical Body.

6. To speak to my pupils of eternity not as an hypothesis that is vague and far off, but as a near and certain reality.

7. To insist on the eternal repercussion of our acts, even of our interior acts.

8. To accustom children to think and speak of the things of eternity as of things intimate and familiar.

9. To recall often that Jesus is the center of all hearts, in whom we shall find again all those whom we love.

PRAYER

Lord Jesus, I am nothing, I have no right to anything, for I have pained You so often. But since in Your goodness You have drawn me out of nothingness that I might be made one with You in eternity, help me to understand the true meaning of death, my birthday in eternity. May the thought of possessing You one day in heaven make me more generous in the accomplishment of Your will in the least details of my daily life. But above all, may the desire to save souls, while there is still time, stimulate my zeal and my charity in Your service for the salvation of souls.

AMEN

Notes

CHAPTER I

¹ *The Religious Vocation*, translated by the Earl of Wicklow (New York: P. J. Kenedy & Sons, 1955).
² *The Humble Virgin Mary* (London: Burns, Oates and Washbourne, Ltd., 1935), p. 94.
³ *Living in God* (Westminster, Maryland: The Newman Press, 1954), pp. 21, 22.
⁴ *Soeur Claire de Jésus, Religieuse Bénédictine*, pp. 122, 179.
⁵ *The Story of a Soul* (Westminster, Maryland: The Newman Press, 1955), pp. 141, 99.

CHAPTER II

¹ *Le trésor des âmes.*
² *Living in God*, p. 12.

CHAPTER III

[1] *The Imitation of Christ,* translated by Abbot Justin McCann (Westminster, Maryland: The Newman Press, 1952), Bk. II, Chap. I, 8.

[2] *Ibid.,* Bk. III, Chap. I, 1.

CHAPTER IV

[1] Thomas Merton, *Seeds of Contemplation* (New York: New Directions, 1949), Chap. IV.

CHAPTER V

[1] Marcelle Auclair, *Teresa of Avila,* translated by Kathleen Pond (New York: Pantheon, 1953), p. 428.

CHAPTER VI

[1] Encyclical *Maximum Illud*
[2] Encyclical *Rerum Ecclesiae*
[3] *Ibid.*
[4] Pierre Charles, S.J., *Prière Missionaire,* p. 7.

CHAPTER VII

[1] Cf. "Quiétisme," *Dictionnaire de Théologie Catholique.*

[2] Allocution at Assisi at the time of the pilgrimage of *Pax Christi,* September 10, 1952.

[3] Quoted in *Pensées et maximes,* collected and edited by Léopold Levaux (Paris-Bruxelles: Éditions Universitaires).

[4] *Living in God,* pp. 10–11.

[5] Quoted in Raoul Plus, S.J., *Une âme de lumière et d'énergie* (Paris: Beauchesne, 1930), p. 70.

[6] *La Réponse du Seigneur,* pp. 170, 285. In the same book one finds (on p. 182) the beautiful definition: ". . . to pray is to contemplate, and to contemplate is to grow."

[7] "Éducation pour la Guerre ou pour la Paix?" *Éducateurs* (Paris: Éditions Fleurus), p. 103.

[8] Cf. M. Guérin-Desjardins, "Pour une compréhension entre les

peuples," and M. l'Abbé Pihan, "Éducation du sens international au catéchisme," in *Éducateurs*.

[9] The Secretariat of *Pax Christi* is at 5 Rue Mabillon, Paris VIe, France.

CHAPTER VIII

[1] Maurice Zundel, *L'Évangile Intérieur* (Paris: Éd. Desclée de Brouwer), pp. 150–155.

A NOTE ON THE TYPE

IN WHICH THIS BOOK IS SET

This book is set in Baskerville, an Intertype face, created from the original types used by John Baskerville, the eighteenth-century typefounder and printer. This type has long been considered one of the finest book types ever developed. The letters are wide and open and have a businesslike approach. The finer hairlines give exquisite delicacy. The heavier strokes give color and strength. The relation of the two in combination gives a brilliant effect and makes for easy reading. The book was composed and printed by the York Composition Company, Inc., of York, Pa., and bound by Moore and Company of Baltimore. The typography and design of the book are by Howard N. King.